TECHNOLOGY FOR
THE REST OF US

TECHNOLOGY FOR THE REST OF US

A Primer on Computer Technologies
for the Low-Tech Librarian

EDITED BY NANCY COURTNEY

LIBRARIES
UNLIMITED
A Member of the Greenwood Publishing Group

Westport, Connecticut • London

Library of Congress Cataloging-in-Publication Data
Technology for the rest of us : a primer on computer technologies for the low-tech librarian / edited by Nancy Courtney.
    p. cm.
Includes bibliographical references and index.
ISBN 1–59158–233–4 (alk. paper)
1. Libraries—Information technology. 2. Libraries—Technological innovations. 3. Library information networks. 4. Telecommunication in libraries. I. Courtney, Nancy.
Z678.9.T415   2005
025'.00285—dc22   2005018009

British Library Cataloguing in Publication Data is available.

Library of Congress Catalog Card Number: 2005018009
ISBN: 1–59158–233–4

First published in 2005

Libraries Unlimited, 88 Post Road West, Westport, CT 06881
A Member of the Greenwood Publishing Group, Inc.
www.lu.com

Printed in the United States of America

The paper used in this book complies with the Permanent Paper Standard issued by the National Information Standards Organization (Z39.48–1984).

10 9 8 7 6 5 4 3 2

CONTENTS

INTRODUCTION

There can be no doubt that computer technology has had a transformative effect on library operations over the last 20 years. We have progressed from online catalogs to computerized indexes and abstracts and now e-journals, ebooks, and even electronic methods of communication with our patrons through chat and e-mail reference services. Networking and the Internet have made it possible for many patrons to complete entire library transactions, from consulting with a librarian to reading the actual material obtained, without setting foot in the library. Although librarians have been enthusiastic early adopters of technology (many academic librarians were among the first users of e-mail on their campuses), training for librarians on technological topics has lagged, especially for the librarian whose primary job responsibilities are not in information technology. In many libraries, computer training is limited to functional courses on word processing, spreadsheets, and presentation software and never addresses higher-level computing topics like networking. Thus, we have a situation in which librarians are affected by technology in every aspect of their jobs but often have little understanding of the technologies underlying the systems they use every day.

Every librarian, no matter how "low-tech" his or her position seems to be, needs to have a basic understanding of computer technologies. For example, computer-security measures adopted by an information technology (IT) department can have serious policy implications for our patrons. IT departments frequently have different service values than librarians. How can we speak intelligently to our technical staffs in order to achieve a balance between security and service without a sound basic understanding of the technologies involved?

This book began as a seminar entitled "Technology for the Rest of Us: What Every Librarian Should Understand about the Technologies that Affect Us" that was held in Columbus, Ohio, May 24–27, 2004. The audience was academic librarians throughout Ohio who were in non-IT positions but who wanted to improve their understanding of technical issues so that they could better participate in library policy and services development. The idea was not to make them IT practitioners but to improve their technological literacy about basic topics that affect libraries, such as networking and computer security, as well as more specific topics that are currently of interest in the library community, such as institutional repositories and OpenURL. Some of the topics and authors in this volume came directly from the seminar, while others were added specifically for this book. It is hoped that readers will find this book a useful and understandable introduction to computer technologies and that they will be encouraged to continue to increase their knowledge of technology topics for the benefit of themselves and their libraries.

Nancy Courtney

1

COMPUTER NETWORKS

Robert E. Molyneux

This chapter is an introduction to computer networks and associated technology for people who will be working as information professionals. The subject is complex, as a visit to a bookstore will show. There are numerous books on various aspects of networks, including hardware, software, and networking protocols, but it is not necessary to know everything there is to know about these networks to be able to use them effectively—nor is it even possible. It is also likely that you know more about networking than you think you know because you use different kinds of networks every day, and these have in common with computer-communications networks concepts that you already understand. As mentioned, the purpose of this chapter is to provide an introduction to the basics of computer networks. Toward that end, I will cover the following:

- Terminology
- Network concepts
- Network characteristics
- The OSI Reference Model, which provides a unifying concept behind these networks
- Digital and analog signals
- The Internet
- Further reading

TERMINOLOGY

Computer networks use many of the same concepts found in highway or airplane or other kinds of networks but often use different words to name these concepts or use the same words in different ways. If you are going to be talking to the folks who work on your networks, you will need to give this matter some thought, because they talk a different language that has its own vocabulary. I usually recommend two print glossaries: Freedman's *Computer Desktop Encyclopedia* and *Newton's Telecom Dictionary*. Freedman has several books with similar titles, and they are excellent for beginners. Newton's is not an introductory glossary, but it is a fine source of information. In addition to these printed sources, Web pages featuring glossaries of networking terms have been cited at the end of the chapter.

Much of this chapter is based on my *Internet Under the Hood*, an introductory book for information professionals on networking and the Internet that addresses both the technology and other issues related to these technologies and changes they have made in our world.

NETWORK CONCEPTS

We have many networks in our lives. We have social networks of friends and business associates, and we travel to see them on physical networks of roads or those run by airlines. We e-mail, talk, surf the Web, or download upgrades to software over computer networks, and our computers are powered by electricity that comes to us over the power grid, which is also a network. The various kinds of networks have common design aspects because they do similar kinds of things, but there are also differences depending on the characteristics of the networks and what they are used for.

According to the *Oxford English Dictionary*, the word *network* first appeared in the English language in the 1565 Geneva Bible. Exodus 27:4, in describing the design of an altar, referred to a "network of brasse." The Hebrew word *reshnet* means a "mesh" or "lattice," and networks are often represented as meshes with crisscrossing connections much like a mesh screen.

To make the concepts presented here clearer, it will be useful to define four terms: *channels, nodes, segments,* and *switches.* By beginning with simple terms, we can bring out network similarities.

Networks are used to move things: people, cars, water, or power. This traffic flows through channels from a source to a destination. The sources and destinations are nodes, and nodes are connected by parts of channels called segments. There are also special nodes called switches. A switch is a place where channels connect and through which traffic from the various segments moves as it passes through the network channel from the source node to the destination node. See Figure 1.1 for a general diagram of a simple network.

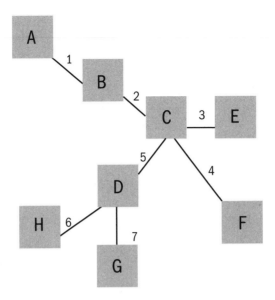

Figure 1.1 A Simple Network

In this network, we have nodes A through H connected by various segments. We see the segments numbered: 1, 2, and so forth. Traffic on our network that is moving from nodes A to F, would go through nodes B and C and travel over segments 1, 2, and 4. These various segments and nodes comprise the whole channel from A to F. Note that traffic going from E to H would travel over segments 3, 5, and 6 and use nodes C and D. So, node C acts as a switch to move traffic between segments and is on both of these different channels (A to F and E to H). In fact, switching will occur at B, C, and D. C is an important node because of its central location in the network.

If this were a highway network, the channels would make up the highway system, and we could think of the channels being broken up into various roads and streets that we might call by their route numbers. The nodes could be cities. You would use maps or the directions of friends to find your way on an unfamiliar set of roads to a destination ("When you get to C, turn right.") If this were an air-traffic network, the nodes would represent airports, and we could think of the segments as routes through the sky connecting various airports in what is referred to as a hub-and-spoke design.

NETWORK CHARACTERISTICS

This section discusses characteristics of networks such as structure (full mesh, partial mesh) and network type (car, airplane, train, data).

Network Structure

A full-mesh network is one in which every network device is connected to every other one. Real networks rarely use the full-mesh topology; most often they will use a partial-mesh design.

Well, why not connect everything? Of course, we could try to connect all devices to all other devices. If we have two computers, we can use one wire to connect them, and if we add another computer, we now need to connect the new one to the two others, so we now have three wires connecting the three computers. What happens if we add another computer? We have the three connected already, but the new node on our budding network has to be connected to each of those three by a separate wire so we now have six wires. But what happens if we have a company with 100 computers and we wish to connect them using this topology? We would need 4,950 wires. Imagine what the device that holds 100 wires to connect to your computer would look like. Every time we added a new computer, we would have to connect it to every other computer.

Suppose the phone network were full mesh? Every time anyone in the country got a new phone, it would have to be connected to all other phones in the country. A full-mesh highway network would result in a large number of roads and continual paving as new houses are added, but, when you were going to drive somewhere, you would set your trusty GPS navigation system to where you need to go and probably just go straight to your destination because so much of the country would have been paved. Wow, think of how much gasoline this design would save! Wouldn't that be great?

But...where would everyone live? Not to speak of the potential for collisions as cars careen around with no highways or stoplights. Add other kinds of networks to the mix (irrigation, trains, airplanes) and our lives would be a chaos of intersecting goods and material if we did not use a tool like networks and keep the movement of those things we need in our daily lives in specialized channels.

So, a partial-mesh network saves us from the nuisance of every kind of network intruding into all aspects of our lives. The network channels can be confined, and network traffic controlled and optimized.

The full-mesh design is typically only used in small applications for reasons that should be clear, so partial-mesh designs are used instead because they have the advantages of the mesh design—multiple connections that allow different routes for network traffic to flow through. If I drive from Washington, DC, to San Francisco, I have the choice of many routes, unlike the small number in our example network. I could decide to drive through New Orleans if there is a snowstorm in St. Louis and could make the decision while already on the road because the network of highways would have many connections to choose from. That is, I could adapt the route I drove in response to changing conditions. I would not be able to go straight, as

I could if the Earth were paved over, but I have the advantages of many connections allowing considerable choice, which allows considerable choice while still letting people go about their daily business without having to live under asphalt.

Why not build a channel directly from A to H in Figure 1.1? One reason is cost: connecting everything on most kinds of networks would be expensive, and maybe the network channels used to get from A to H are good enough for the purpose of the network. Networks are tools that cost money, so there are compromises brought on by practical considerations such as costs. Network engineers would monitor the traffic moving from A to H and may decide in the future to add a channel if the traffic warranted it or for other reasons, such as security. Part of the specialty of networks is the specialized monitoring of them. Not that that always matters. One thing that happened during the dot.com boom was that too much network cable was laid, resulting in substantial overcapacity, even before technical developments made it possible to get huge increases in capacity out of existing cable.

In the real world, the paths in Figure 1.1 and the traffic that flows over them can be of many types, depending on what is moving on the network.

Network Terms

Networks of all types have similarities and often-similar terminology.

Networks channel traffic and those channels have measures of the capacity they can handle and rates measuring actual traffic over them. Road traffic can be measured in cars per hour, irrigation networks have a flow rate that measures number of gallons per unit of time, and in data networks we use the term *bandwidth* to describe a network's capacity and measures of speed, such as "10 megabits per second (mbps)."

If we do move traffic by a network, that traffic must be able to move or switch (as we saw happens at B, C, and D) from one of the segments to another on its journey Thus, there is a place or device that does the switching, and these devices have different names depending on the kind of traffic, but several of these names are reused from one type of network to another.

Highways employ cloverleafs and intersections to switch cars between various roads; computer networks have hubs, switches, and routers; airlines and cable TV networks also have hubs; trains have stations and switches; and Washington DC's Metro, for example, has a Metro Center where a number of lines intersect and people switch between those lines. Telephone networks, too, have switches. The switching used to be done by operators, who manually switched voice traffic carried over the wires of the phone networks that connected the phones of customers. If you picked up a phone in early phone networks, you would get the operator and you would ask her to connect you with the person you wanted to talk to ("Mabel, can I have June Smith?") and the operator would connect your line with her line by plugging wires directly into the switchboard. Train switches used to be manual, too. Network switch-ing on almost all networks is now automatic or controlled by machines.

These days, the telephone switches are computers and are capable of switching voice traffic across the world automatically. It all starts with your local Central Office (CO)—a local switch in your neighborhood that handles the local traffic and puts the traffic on higher-speed lines. The local segment is called, in phone parlance, the local loop. If you call your next-door neigh-bor, the call is switched from your line to his line at the CO. If your call is going to Sheboygan, the call will be sent through a series of switches from your local loop over high-speed lines to the CO of the person you are calling. Internet traffic moves through various devices and media in an astonishingly complex array that is often referred to as the cloud because, well, it is so cloudy to most of us and normally we do not have to worry our pretty little heads about it. But the more you know about it, the more you will see that it is both complex and a magnificent achievement.

The various networks also have rules to ensure the orderly flow of traffic. In computer networks protocols handle this function. Protocols are the rules followed in networks. Similar protocols exist in other network types too. In traffic networks we have rules about acceptable behavior, such as speed lim-its, and devices, such as lights and stop signs, that perform the function of regulating the orderly flow of traffic. If you are used to driving in the United States and visit the UK, you are reminded of the cost of driving on the incor-rect side of the road, because they have a workable protocol but one that is different. For this traffic protocol, it does not matter which we do as long as everyone within a country does the same thing. This protocol attempts to prevent collisions of cars. In traffic networks we talk about the "right of way" and in data networks we talk of media-access control—which machine or traffic controls the medium (that is, the segment) the signal travels on and has the right to send on the network. In other words, which machine has the green light to control the segment at a given time?

The Transmission Control Protocol and the Internet Protocol are often referred to as "TCP/IP" in network jargon, a metonymy to indicate all the various protocols that make up the Internet and to distinguish them from all the other network protocols. Most networks these days run more than one set of network protocols at one time, and part of managing a network is to make sure all those protocols play nice with each other.

Network Architectures

These different network types share other structural aspects besides switches and protocols—they also have common architectures. We have already seen partial and full mesh, of course, but there are others.

In road networks, the Interstate system has higher capacity than the road in your neighborhood, and low-capacity commuter airlines ("feeders") connect small airports, while large-capacity airplanes fly between hub airports. In our network in Figure 1.1, the connection between C and D is likely to have a higher capacity than that between A and B, but, if there is a lot of traffic between A and B, the traffic engineers (be they highway or network engineers or whatever other kind of network-traffic engineer) would increase the capacity of this connection. Or if A were particularly important—suppose this were a company network and the payroll computer were at A, the network engineers might provide another connection to the rest of the network by running a line to D to avoid a "single point of failure" and to make it less likely that paychecks would be interrupted. But, typically, traffic is gathered from low-speed parts of the network and is aggregated for the main roads or high-speed channels, and when it gets near its destination, it is routed through slower channels to its destination. We are all familiar with the phenomenon of the drive home from the airport taking as long as the flight as a result of this aspect of the transportation network.

Network Glitches

There are tradeoffs in networks and engineers work to take them into account.

There is a tradeoff between efficiency and robustness and if you get it wrong, it can make the newspapers. Consider the airline network. The hub-and-spoke design for locating airports is efficient in good weather and the air-traffic control system works relatively well in those conditions, but a bit of bad weather can cause the airplane network to falter because is not robust when things go wrong. This fact occurs for several reasons. One is the inefficiency of the air-traffic control system, which still uses primitive vacuum tubes and which forces airlines into highways in the sky, thus making it impossible to have planes go straight to the destination—a inherent impossibility in a car network, but not in the airline network. When something does go wrong, collapse is quick and it is difficult to get the network working again—given the daily rhythm of travel, it normally takes at least until the next morning, sometimes longer, by which time air traffic has backed up, to restore normal traffic flow.

Traffic backs up on the Internet, too, and when it is, it is stored temporarily in areas called buffers or caches, which are like dams that hold data instead of water. Data traffic can be discarded if the buffers become full—something the airlines cannot do with their airplanes' contents—that is, you and me. The plane buffer leads to upset passengers in airline terminals often sleeping on floors. Highway buffers in the mornings and evenings are called rush hour, and take the form of turning commuter highways into parking lots. In order to make networks more robust, they are designed to correct for congestion if possible.

As mentioned, network buffers act as dams to accumulate traffic, and these dams have a means of gathering and holding excess traffic, but they also throw traffic away when they get overloaded. Because these systems are increasingly automated, when one of these control machines makes a spectacular mistake, we read about it in the newspaper or sit in the dark because of a power blackout and wonder, "Where is it all headed?"

Computer Networks Today

There are, then, characteristics that are common to different kinds of networks, but communications networks form a subset of all networks and here commonalities are a result of their handling traffic with a similar purpose, although the traffic can be of different types. These different kinds of traffic necessitate different kinds of designs and hardware and resulted in different histories. Historically, there are three types of communications networks that concerned us most: voice, video, and data; today all three are converging into one: the Internet. You will read about VoIP (Voice over the Internet Protocol) as companies have begun offering inexpensive telephone service using the Internet as opposed to the traditional phone network. There are even articles about "everything over IP." Everything will not go over IP—yet— but not many people are betting against that eventuality. Records in libraries, too, are converging to the same hard drives whether those records are sound, text, or pictures.

Most modern data-communication networks are built with combinations of the Ethernet protocols for local area network (LAN) traffic and the Internet protocols, our friend TCP/IP, for both LAN and wide area network (WAN) traffic. Roughly, a LAN is something your organization controls, but you usually are in the WAN business when the backhoes are brought in. The adopting of Ethernet and TCP/IP is recent and may well change. After all, the one constant in networks is change.

What are of central interest to information professionals, though, are the records of the human species that hold the information that these networks are used to store and move. At one time, these records were in a variety of formats—paper, vinyl records, hand-copied manuscripts and papyrus, stone, canvas, clay tablets, glass—but convergence also applies to the fact that, increasingly, human records are produced digitally and old records are being converted to digital formats. The digitization of the human record is occurring because digital formats are superior to many of the older formats for many—though not all—purposes. However, not all of these records yet have formats that can be stored as digital records. I will return to what we mean by "digital" in the section "Digital and Analog Signals."

THE OSI REFERENCE MODEL

A key to understanding computer networks is found in the OSI (Open System Interconnection) Reference Model of network design.

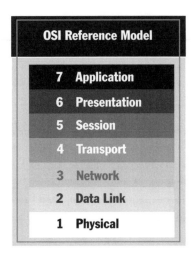

Figure 1.2 OSI Reference Model

The diagram in Figure 1.2 is a theoretical and engineering conception of communications networks and was developed and finally published in 1984 by the International Organization for Standardization.

Most networking protocols have similar models—the Internet, in fact, uses a different model—but no matter which protocols you or they work with, you will be able to talk with network colleagues using the language of this model because all sets of networking protocols use the OSI model as a means of describing what they do. It is often referred to as a reference model because other networking protocols use it for comparison and for teaching purposes.

It also has a lesson about people and networks. As is true of so much about networking, the engineering aspects have a human dimension. As you move around the networking world, you will find that different people specialize in either the machinery, protocols, or applications necessary to the smooth functioning of different layers. Each involves its own technologies, is complex, and requires different skills. People specialize in layers, in other words, especially at places with big networks.

Part of the problem of the new information professional is to find that part of this complex undertaking that he or she wants to specialize in—or, indeed, if he or she wishes to specialize at all. You can think of these layers as a clue to the kinds of specialties available in networking. People may be drawn to the tasks, problems, and methods of a particular layer and end up working in what interests them. Information professionals, though, may end up working in areas where there is a broader picture: not setting up routers or pulling cable but having to ask, Where is this all going? What is the reason we are creating this network? There is a lot to do and a lot of places to do it. I have often referred to a fictional "Layer 8" in talking to students, because in libraries the decisions about what the networks will be used for is a function decided outside the OSI Model—it is related to what the mission of the institution is and how networks can advance that mission.

What the layers do:

- 7—*Application layer.* Manages what the user sees. Has functions for applications like browsers.
- 6—*Presentation layer.* Formats received files for the user. Translates file formats and makes sense of such things as .jpg and .wav files.
- 5—*Session layer.* Handles opening, maintaining, and closing connections.
- 4—*Transport layer.* Controls end-to-end communications, ensures delivery of packets.
- 3—*Network layer.* Deals with routing and addressing. Gets packets between machines.
- 2—*Data Link layer.* Controls errors from the Physical layer and imposes meaning on the bits received from it. Provides a stable layer for upper-level protocols.
- 1—*Physical layer.* Moves bits over the network medium. Ensures accurate signaling.

There are practical aspects of such models that will become clear in the pages that will follow:

- The various layers are modular. If one is changed, the others can function as before. That is, if you replace your dial-up Internet connection with a broadband connection, you do not have to change your PC or its operating system or the browser you use to surf the Web.
- The layers function independently and cooperatively. The Data Link layer does what it does without any understanding of what the Network layer does, and the Network layer has no notion of what the upper layers or the Data Link layer do. This fact is largely true of each layer, but they must cooperate and communicate with each other if networks are to work. This fact is also true of the various people in networking who work on different layers. If you like to work with layer 2, you will likely regard layer 3 concerns as esoteric but you will know how to ensure that traffic gets handed off to layer 3 devices correctly.

What each layer does and how it does it varies with the networking protocols. Each is different and is established by various standards and protocols.

DIGITAL AND ANALOG SIGNALS

Signals are what layer 1 is about.

Although voice and video networks share many characteristics, historically, the telephone voice network was responsible for the initial research and development of our communications networks, and data networks often started out using phone technology—for instance, coaxial cable, a phone-company invention, was the first medium used for Ethernet networks. Research was conducted at Bell Labs, in New Jersey, among other places and the result was a well-engineered network that would eventually supply the initial infrastructure to data networks. However, this phone technology did not prove suitable for data networks.

Historically, the phone network was analog, but it is now a mix of digital (for the long-haul parts of the network) and analog for the local loop and to your ears. Your ears are analog devices, so what is hooked up to you will be analog. But what is an "analog" signal?

Analog signals are continuous wave forms (see Figure 1.3). Sound is the result of the motion of waves in air or water. You cannot hear in space because there is no medium to convey the sound waves. By modulating, or changing the wave form, you can change the sound you hear.

Digital signals, however, have a simpler structure and have two values, represented here as 1's and 0's (see Figure 1.4). In a computer network, these 1's and 0's are grouped in packets, which are rather like envelopes, each separately addressed with where they come from and where they are going. Data networks are frequently referred to as packet-switched networks, while the phone network was circuit-switched (at least historically), because when I called you there was an identifiable circuit from me to you, whereas my e-mail to you might be broken up in 100 packets that might well go by 25 different routes through the cloud to you. And when that e-mail gets to you, you are not able to read it without a machine to decode the 1's and 0's.

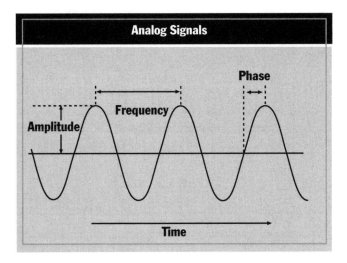

Figure 1.3 An Analog Signal

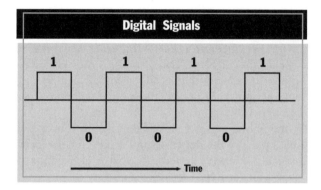

Figure 1.4 A Digital Signal

In fact, we always need a device of some kind to take digital signals and put them in a form we can use.

Now, why in the world are we moving our records and communications from something you can use without a machine to something that requires a machine to interpret? The short version of the answer is that digital signaling is better on a computer network than analog signaling, as the Bell System found when it invented a form of digital signaling. As signals travel on networks, they break down and grow weaker and noise is introduced into the network, so the signals have to be regenerated and amplified. We have no technology to amplify and clean up noise in analog signals well enough to make it practical, whereas amplifying and cleaning up digital signals is relatively simple—after all, you merely have to decide if something is a 1 or a 0.

That is the short version and the long version is more complex but fascinating.

The revolution we are in, though, can be looked at as the conversion of the human record from all other formats to digital formats and the conversion of data-communications networks to digital networks. Today, in almost all forms of human expression and record keeping, the process of converting the output of our species—our records, data, music, poetry, and other forms of expression—to media and formats that can be created, manipulated, and stored using computers is proceeding at a furious pace.

THE INTERNET

The Internet forms a backdrop of our notions about what computer networks are used for. The Internet communications protocols have become the preferred method for sending data on communications networks, particularly over long distances. There are historical and technical factors behind this rapid growth but for now consider how fast our notion of the Internet has grown since the invention of the World Wide Web, which is built on just one of the Internet protocols (the Hypertext Transport Protocol, or HTTP), but the one that caught the imagination of the world and has spread so rapidly.

In the early days before HTTP, the Internet protocols file transfer protocol (FTP) and the Internet Terminal Emulation Protocol (telnet) were used by increasing numbers of people, but they required an above-average understanding of computers to use them. Gopher, introduced in 1991, is a text-based and menu-driven Internet protocol that led to the first explosion of Internet use. Gopher did not require the user to be very knowledgeable about computers because the technical infrastructure was hidden. Teaching Internet classes at the time usually involved leading students reluctantly through FTP and telnet. Their interest had picked up with e-mail, but with Gopher the room would get quiet as people started wandering where their tastes and interests took them. They were caught in the wonder of readily available information without having to enter arcane commands: they could just browse. It was magic. The first time most people saw Gopher, their world changed. It was something commensurate to our capacity for wonder.

The invention of HTTP by Tim Berners-Lee (also released in 1991) and the 1993 release of Mosaic by Marc Andreesen at the National Center for Supercomputer Applications at the University of Illinois led to the explosion that continues today. Mosaic solved a nagging problem with Gopher and with text-based Web browsers such as the program *Lynx*. While Gopher was easy to use with text, multimedia files (sound and pictures among other formats) still required knowledge and effort on the part of the user. Mosaic solved that problem by being the first graphical Web browser; therefore it was easy to use and could display pictures and sound. It was revolutionary. When it was released, the program was seemingly everywhere in a short period of time, and the Web's use soon dwarfed the use of all other Internet protocols. For all practical purposes, Gopher is gone but if you ever run across a Gopher server, your Web browser will be able to read its files.

It is hard to believe that so much has happened since 1993, and students new to the Internet think that the Web is the Internet. It is not. The Web is a recent development in communications networks and more are on the way; it is just the networking development that caught the imagination of the world and put the promise of computer networks and abundant and available information within the reach of most people.

FURTHER READING

Learning networking is like learning a second language: "technology as a second language." The first thing you will need is a guide to that language. I recommend two glossaries:

Freedman, Alan. (1999). *Computer desktop encyclopedia* (2nd ed.). New York: AMACOM. ISBN: 0–8144–7985–5.

This book provides excellent general explanations and definitions of most common computer terms. Various other dictionaries by Freedman have been published, but this is the best developed so far.

Newton, Harry. (2001). *Newton's telecom dictionary* (17th ed.). New York: CMP Books. ISBN: 1–57820–069–5.

This book is for a more technical audience than Freedman's, but it is invaluable and a highly regarded book in communications networks and in both in voice and data-communications networks.

For students starting out, these glossaries are excellent. But, what if you want to know just a bit more on a topic? This book provides a good next source:

Sheldon, Tom. (2001). *Encyclopedia of networking and telecommunications.* Berkeley, CA: Osborne/McGraw Hill. ISBN: 0–07–212005–3. There is a related Web site at URL: http://www.linktionary.com/

And there is my introductory book on the world of the Internet and networking:

Molyneux, Robert E. (2003). *Internet under the hood: An introduction to network technologies for information professionals.* Westport, CT: Libraries Unlimited. ISBN: 1–59158–005–6

Web sites

Acronym and Abbreviation Server. (URL: http://www.ucc.ie/info/net/acronyms/
    acro.html)
TechWeb's Tech Encyclopedia. (URL: http://www.techweb.com/encyclopedia/)
Webopedia. (URL: http://webopedia.internet.com/)

2

─◆─

WIRELESS LOCAL AREA NETWORKS
Wilfred Drew, Jr.

McDonald's, Barnes & Noble, Starbucks, Borders, LaGuardia International Airport, Best Western, Sheraton, Marriott. What do all of these locations have in common? They all provide access to Wireless Local Area Networks (WLANs), commonly called either wireless or Wi-Fi (short for "Wireless Fidelity"). If McDonald's and Borders can provide areas covered by wireless—also known as hotspots—why can't your library? Are you afraid of the costs or are you unable to think of why you should be doing it?

There are many reasons for implementing wireless in your library. Wireless allows for flexible configuration of rooms through the use of laptops. Patrons can work wherever they want in a space covered by a WLAN and can bring in their own wireless devices. It can result in greater productivity for your staff and improved service to your patrons. Patrons and staff will be able to access networked resources during meetings. You will be able to provide printing from anywhere in the library. You can also place computers where needed, not just where there is wire. Wireless service will allow reference staff to roam and still have access to network and library resources.

It is not even particularly expensive. Cost per seat can be lower than adding ports to a wired network; wireless kits can be purchased at Wal-Mart for $60 Also, installation can be very fast. All that is required is a port connected to your broadband connection and electrical power.

A WLAN enables your device to stay connected to your wired network without a wire or cable. WLANs can use infrared light, lasers, or radio signals to connect to the wired network. Most WLANs use radio waves. We will focus on that.

HISTORY AND STANDARDS

As a technology, radio has been around for many years. Marconi started experimenting with radio in 1894. Five years later, the first signals were transmitted across the Atlantic. Other advances soon followed. The first TV broadcast was in 1939. In 1942 the movie actress Hedy Lamarr and the composer George Antheil came up with the basic idea for frequency hopping, or spread-spectrum technology, that modern cell phone and WLANs are based on. The first WLAN was deployed in 1971 in the Hawaiian Islands. It was based on technology (packet radio) developed by the Allies and the U.S. Army during World War II to transmit and receive encrypted data. The 1971 use connected seven computers on four islands together and was call ALOH-NET ("Tom's Networking," 2004). The next big event was the introduction of the first cellular phone system in 1977. It was constructed by AT&T and Bell Labs. The first trials of a commercial cellular phone system were set up in Chicago in 1978, with over 2,000 customers (Bellis, 2004). At the same time that wireless technologies were developing, new computer technologies led to the introduction of laptop computers and personal digital devices (PDAs) in the 1990s.

The most important event in the growth of WLANs was the adoption in 1997 of the Institute of Electrical and Electronics Engineers (IEEE) 802.11 Standard for WLANs. This standard describes the protocols and sets a common framework for all developers. It was followed in 1999 by 802.11b and 802.11a. 802.11b is the most widely used currently. The most up to date wireless setups are based on the IEEE 802.11b or 802.11a or 802.11g standards. If you are purchasing new equipment, make sure it meets the IEEE 802.11g standard and is Wi-Fi certified by the Wi-Fi Alliance, because 802.11g provides greater bandwidth and is compatible with the common 802.11b standard. The Wi-Fi Alliance (www.wirelessethernet.org) was organized to "certify interoperability of wireless Local Area Network products based on IEEE 802.11 specification." It provides the latest information on compatibility and a list of Wi-Fi certified products. Wi-Fi certification ensures that you can buy Access Points and Network Interface Cards from different manufacturers as long as they all have the Wi-Fi stamp of approval (Wi-Fi Alliance, 2004).

Wireless standards are used so that manufacturers can produce devices that will talk with each other no matter what the brand. 802.11 includes several standards, each designated with a letter of the alphabet:

- 802.11a: This is not as widely used as 820.11b. The 5 GHz range is not available in every country. Parts of it are controlled by the military. 802.11a also competes with other uses for that part of the radio-frequency space.
- 802.11b: 11 Mbps, 2.4 GHz, most popular.
- 802.11e: Quality of Service for voice and -full motion video.

- 802.11f: Similar to Wi-Fi compatibility.
- 802.11g: Higher Data rate (>20 Mbps), 2.4GHz. Will be most widely used.
- 802.11i: Authentication and security.

HOW DOES A WLAN WORK?

A WLAN uses radio waves in the 2.4 to 5 Gigahertz (GHz) range to send and receive signals among its various components. The Access Point (AP) is a transmitter/receiver that acts as a connection between wireless clients and wired networks. It is generally plugged directly into an Ethernet port in the local wired network. Ethernet is the network-communication standard for wired local area networks. It communicates with the user's device, such as a PDA, laptop computer, or even a cellular phone, via a Network Interface Card (NIC). The NIC is hardware installed in the user's device that enables it to communicate on a network using radio waves since it is a radio transmitter and receiver. A typical NIC for a laptop computer fits in one of the personal computer manufacturer interface adapter (PCMIA) slots. It may look like a credit card with an antenna connected to it.

In a typical installation, a library patron walks in with his personal laptop that has wireless capabilities. The NIC in the laptop searches the area for a signal from the AP. The AP checks to see if the patron meets its requirements for accessing the network. If he does, the AP sends back the necessary information to the NIC and the connection is negotiated and established. The patron is now on the network and connected. As the patron walks around the library, he searches the online public access catalog (OPAC). He finds a book he is interested in and heads for the stacks. As he leaves the lobby of the library for the stacks, he reaches the end of the range of the first AP. His laptop immediately connects with the next AP, and the connection to the network is continued without the patron needing to do anything.

TYPES OF WLANS

There are several possible configurations for WLANs. One type is an informal network in which several devices talk directly to each other via the NICs without the use of APs. This is called peer-to-peer wireless networking. The computers are only talking to each other and have no connection to any other network. Two or more can then talk to each other without a formal network.

Another very simple setup consists of a single AP with one or more clients. A client is any device, such as a computer or laptop, that is connecting to the wireless network. A single AP would be typical of a home wireless network or of that found in a small building.

A more typical setup would consist of multiple APs, which allows users to roam around a building or even go outside of the building. WLANs can also extend between buildings through the use of extension points. An extension point is an AP that receives and transmits a signal to another AP in another building or nearby location. It acts as a bridge to an area without any wired connection to the main network or backbone. The bridge can then be plugged into a wired network in that building or location, providing a connection to the rest of the network.

SECURITY

Security is extremely important for WLANs. They can be vulnerable to hackers and unauthorized access. If you are sending circulation transactions over a wireless network, someone with the right equipment could read the information or get access to areas they should not be in. Besides the security methods available for wired LANs—for example, Virtual Private Networks (VPNs), which authenticate users before allowing them to use the network, and encrypting data being transmitted—WLANs have their own options for network security.

Perhaps the widest-used protocol is the Wired Equivalent Privacy (WEP) algorithm. It is built into most APs. WEP uses what is called a key to encrypt its data. The AP and the wireless client (laptop or other device) use the same key to encrypt and decrypt the data. What this means is that the data cannot be intercepted and understood by the casual user. It allows the data to be put into the equivalent of a locked diplomatic pouch. The pouch can then be opened only by using the correct key. The AP and the client both have that key. WEP is set up by the network administrator in any of various ways, depending on the product purchased. It may require the administrator to physically go to each AP, or it may be set up over the network via a special program or via a Web browser. A typical setup would require the administrator to turn on encryption, since the default is usually having it turned off. Encryption can also usually be set so it is optional, in the event that the client is not capable of using WEP.

The administrator must also check the type of authentication allowed on the AP. If this is set to open key authentication, it allows any device, regardless of its WEP keys, to attempt to authenticate and gain access to the network. While a quick search on Google shows much discussion on Open versus Shared, most experts agree Open is actually more secure than the shared key setting because shared key allows those with the right equipment to acquire data that can be used to calculate the shared key. The shared key setting allows the Access Point to send a plain-text, shared key to any client trying to get access to the network, which is much less secure. Anyone with the proper equipment and programs could then read the key and get access to the network. The administrator must also decide on the length of the key. It can be set to either 40- or 128-bit. 128-bit is more secure. At the same time, the administrator must type in ten hexadecimal digits (any combination of 0–9, a–f, or A–F) for 128-bit keys. The same key must also be entered into every client device and AP across the network. Imagine typing in "64A7BFCFC3104A0B98841C3545" for several dozen APs and possibly hundreds of wireless devices.

WEP has many weaknesses. Because of the difficulty in setting it up, many sites do not bother to change the factory defaults. These defaults are well known to potential abusers of the WLAN. The biggest difficulty is the need to install the same key on the client. Because of this, many administrators may not turn on WEP at all. Other weaknesses are the fact that parts of the WEP process may be transmitted as plain text and encryption is very weak. But WEP is better than nothing.

Recently, there has been an effort by the Wi-Fi Alliance to improve security, Wi-Fi Protected Access (WPA). It is designed to overcome the basic weaknesses of WEP by providing improved encryption of data and by improving authorization routines. It uses a password (preshared key). The key is entered using regular characters. The Wi-Fi Alliance suggests at least a 12-character password. The AP and client use the key to generate new keys on other devices on the network. For equipment manufactured since September 2003, WPA has been a part of Wi-Fi certification. All equipment on the network should meet that certification. Older equipment may require a software update (Wi-Fi Alliance, 2004b).

Improvements in security for WLANs will be available very soon. IEEE just approved 802.11i. It is a vast improvement over WEP. It builds on the strengths of WPA. It uses a security algorithm called Temporal Key Integrity Protocol (TKIP). It provides improved confidentiality, secure recognition of the origin of the data being transmitted or received, and greatly improved authentication. Many are using TKIP as shorthand for 802.11i. 802.11i can also use other, more robust protocols such as Robust Security Network Associations (RSN) or Counter-Mode Cipher Block Chaining Message Authentication Code Protocol (CCMP). Access Points and clients using this new standard are now widely available, according to WindowsSecurity. Com (Shinder, 2004).

By now you are probably asking what you need to do for a secure network. The National Institute of Standards and Technology (Karygiannis and Owens, 2002) recommends the following:

1. Develop a security program. This would include physical security of your AP and full control over who can configure them. The APs at my library are installed in Lucite cases ten to fifteen feet off the floor. The cases require special tools to open them.

2. Have a complete inventory of all access points. Anyone can now purchase a WLAN kit at such chain stores as Wal-Mart or Best Buy for under $100. These rogue APs

will allow others to bypass your security on the network. There are tools available to detect APs over the network.

3. Change default settings on APs. Default WEP and WPA settings are usually set at the lowest level possible by manufacturers.

4. Enable all security features of your WLAN. It is also quite difficult to locate some of these settings for some APs, so many administrators do not bother to turn them on.

5. Use encrypted authentication and VPNs. Use external authentication such as you would require for users accessing their e-mail from your servers.

6. Consider using a firewall between the WLAN and rest of network. Many libraries and other institutions provide a separate network for the WLAN, especially ones set up for public use. Administrative functions are run separately from the WLAN.

PLANNING FOR YOUR NETWORK

Several aspects related to facilities and equipment need to be taken into consideration when planning for your wireless installation. Do not forget that you must have a wired network in order to have a wireless network. Wireless will be slower than your wired LANs (<100 Mbps), since wireless bandwidth is less than that of wired, but it will be more reliable than the wired network because it contains fewer points of failure. WLANs' only points of possible failure are the AP or the NIC. Both can be replaced very easily to troubleshoot the problem.

Wireless allows a user to move from AP to AP through a building without losing connectivity. You need to decide where such areas will be. Compatibility and interoperability are crucial. Be sure that cards you purchase for your computers can talk with the APs. To ensure this, use only Wi-Fi-certified equipment. You need to know the physical structure of your building. Brick and stone can block signals, as can steel or wire mesh used in some construction. What is under that plaster in the lobby? What is in the concrete floor between the second and third stories? Will the microwave oven in the staff lounge need to be moved? Will the signals reach to an area you do not want covered by the network?

Other potential obstacles to planning wireless installations in a library are that few libraries seem to be willing to share their planning experiences and few planning resources are available for libraries. Most books and articles are aimed at business users. More positively, though, since WLAN installation can be quite simple, small libraries may not need to do formal planning if they are installing only one or two APs. Also, many libraries are part of larger institutions and can piggyback on the parent institution's efforts.

GETTING HELP

Now that you know how wireless works and have some ideas about how to plan, you are probably wondering where you can go for help. One place to start is with the LibWireless discussion group (LibWireless, 2004), whose purpose is to discuss libraries and all types of wireless technologies, including, but not limited to, WLANs in libraries, accessing library resources via wireless devices, and related issues such as wireless bookmobiles. To subscribe, use the online form available at the site.

You can also go to my Web site, the Wireless Librarian (Drew, 2004), which includes an article bibliography (with links to full text where available), a book bibliography, and links to libraries that have wireless networks, to vendors, to WLAN consultants, and to other useful resources.

There are two groups that also provide many free documents online. WLANA (Wireless LAN Association) is the trade association for the WLAN industry. It has many useful resources on its Web site at http://www.wlana. org. These include white papers on security, detailed information on WLAN technologies, and other items of interest.

Another valuable source of information is the Web site of the Wi-Fi Alliance, a "nonprofit international association formed in 1999 to certify interoperability of wireless Local Area Network products based on IEEE 802.11 specification. Currently the Wi-Fi Alliance has over 200 member companies from around the world, and over 1500 products have received Wi-Fi® certification since certification began in March of 2000.The goal of the Wi-Fi Alliance's members is to enhance the user experience through product interoperability" (2004). One of the more interesting services provided by the alliance is the Wi-Fi Zone. The Zone provides a free service through which service providers of WLAN "hotspots" that use Wi-Fi certified hardware, such as libraries, can be found. Again, a hotspot is the geographic area covered by a wireless network.

WHAT NEXT?

Once you get your WLAN up and running, what do you do next? One of the best things to do is to let the world know about it. JiWire provides a free search engine for users to locate hotspots around the world (2004). It does not cost anything for libraries to be listed. On my Web site, the Wireless Librarian, I also maintain a directory and offer ideas on how to promote your wireless efforts to your users.

REFERENCES

Bellis, Mary. (2004). Selling the cell phone—Part 1: history of cellular phones. *About.com: Inventors.* URL: http://inventors.about.com/library/weekly/aa070899.htm (Accessed August 19, 2004).

Drew, Wilfred. (2004). The Wireless Librarian. URL: http://people.morrisville. edu/~drewwe/wireless/ (Accessed August 19, 2004).

JiWire. (2004). URL: http://www.jiwire.com (Accessed August 19, 2004)

Karygiannis, Tom, and Owens, Les. (2002). *Wireless network security—802.11, bluetooth and handheld devices.* Special Publication 800–48. Gaithersburg, MD:

National Institute of Standards and Technology, U.S. Department of Commerce. URL: http://people.morrisville.edu/~drewwe/wireless/NIST_SP_800–48.pdf (Accessed August 19, 2004).

LibWireless. (2004). URL: http://people.morrisville.edu/~drewwe/wireless/libwireless.html (Accessed August 19, 2004).

Shinder, Deb. (2004). 802.11i, WPA, RSN and what it all means to wi-fi security. Window Security.Com: Internet Software Marketing Ltd. URL: http://www.windowsecurity.com/articles/80211i-WPA-RSN-Wi-Fi-Security.html (Accessed August 19, 2004).

Tom's networking: wireless local area networking. (2004). Tom's Guides Publishing. URL: http://www.tomsnetworking.com/network/20010822/ (Accessed August 19, 2004).

Wi-Fi Alliance. (2004). URL: http://www.wi-fi.org (Accessed August 19, 2004)

"Wi-Fi Overview." (2004a). Wi-Fi Alliance. URL: http://www.wi-fi.org/Open Section/why_Wi-Fi.asp?TID = 2 (Accessed August 19, 2004).

Wi-Fi Alliance. (2004b). WI-FI PROTECTED ACCESS.URL: http://www.wi-fi.org/OpenSection/pdf/Wi-Fi_Protected_Access_Overview.pdf (Accessed August 19, 2004).

WLANA (Wireless LAN Association). URL: http://www.wlana.org (Accessed July 6, 2005)

3

CYBERTHEFT, NETWORK SECURITY, AND THE LIBRARY WITHOUT WALLS*

Mark Cain

In December, officials at JSTOR, the non-profit agency that for almost a decade has been digitally archiving scholarly journals, reported that it had been the victim of a carefully coordinated theft attempt across the Internet. Apparently this thievery had been underway for some time:

> Toward the end of August we noticed that an IP address at a participating site was downloading a lot of articles—hundreds of complete issues. We denied access to JSTOR from that address and sent a note to our contacts at the site. At this point, we had no reason to think that this was anything other than ordinary "over-enthusiastic" use of the archive. A few days later, another address had a noticeably high number of article downloads, with hundreds of complete issues. So, again, we denied access from the second address and sent a message to our contacts there. Our first indication that something strange was afoot was in their reply. They had contacted the office to which the IP address in question belonged; no one there had been using JSTOR, and the machine that the IP address belonged to was an internal Web server and thus not a workstation from which people typically browsed the Web.[1]

The perpetrators were from another country, and before they were stopped they had succeeded in downloading 50,000 journal articles. While the extent of the theft was less than 5% of JSTOR's digital archives, the intent was clear: the systematic downloading of the entire database, presumably to repackage and sell it.[2]

JSTOR had a specific attack to thwart, which they did, but officials of that organization did not stop there. They did a great deal of research on the

* From Cain, Mark. (2003) "Cybertheft, Network Security, and the Library Without Walls." *Journal of Academic Librarianship* 29 (2): 245-48. Reprinted with permission.

method through which the crime was effected. They went public with the story, informing the news media and their users about the security vulnerability that was exploited in an attempt to keep it from happening to other repositories of digital information. In fact, JSTOR has developed a Web site about the break-in.

How did it happen? Were the criminals world-class hackers who could have broken into any system they wanted, no matter what the security precautions? They could have been, but the method of attack was to use extremely common devices employed by many institutions, ironically, to provide security and enhanced network performance. I'm referring to proxy servers.[3]

SOME NETWORK AND SECURITY BASICS

To understand what proxy servers are and do—and what risks they can pose—requires some basic knowledge of networks, the Internet, and security. A short review is in order.

Networks are combinations of hardware and software that provide for the transport of information. Copper wire, optical fiber, and sometimes radio waves form a network's lines; switches or hubs split those lines up so they can be shared by multiple users. Servers dish up content. The Internet is comprised of pretty much the same items.

Information that travels over networks adheres to certain standards, or protocols. There are many of these. HTTP, or hypertext transport protocol, runs the World Wide Web. File Transfer Protocol (FTP) lets users move files over great distances. Underneath these higher-order standards are some more fundamental network protocols. Local area networks may employ Appletalk (Macintosh), NetBUI (Windows), or some other communication standards, but if those networks are going to talk to the Internet, they must also support TCP/IP. (More and more networks just use TCP/IP; it's more efficient than running multiple standards.) TCP/IP is in fact a suite of protocols, but it has two main parts. The Transmission Control Protocol (TCP) disassembles information into smaller packets. These packets travel across networks and the Internet, in theory along many different paths, depending upon which are the most efficient at any given moment, and then get reassembled on the other end.

The second part of TCP/IP is the Internet Protocol (IP). IP provides the addresses, so the packets know where to go. These addresses are either hard-coded, that is, a specific address typed into the software defining a computer's network properties, or dynamically and temporarily assigned to the computer by a server. This latter technique is called Dynamic Host Configuration Protocol, or DHCP. DHCP is what is typically used on networks because of the flexibility it provides. However, hard-coded, or static, IP addresses are still frequently used for networked devices, like switches and servers, including proxy servers. An IP address, whether hard-coded or temporarily assigned, must be unique, that is, there should be no two devices in the networked world with the same address. (This is a simplification but is basically correct.)

An IP address consists of four numbers separated by periods. The numbers between the periods can be anywhere from 0 to 255 and look something like this:

255.0.255.10

The IP address a machine has, or appears to have, bears directly on the resources it may access. Because of this, IP figures prominently in securing networked resources.

In a perfect world, network security wouldn't exist. It's a barrier and, generally speaking, has an inverse relationship with functionality. Librarians and other users of information systems usually find network security to be a nuisance. But just as we understand we should lock our cars when we leave them in parking lots, so we know that we must secure our networks.

A common method of doing so is to use firewalls. These are systems comprising hardware and/or software. They usually sit between an institution's network and the Internet, though they can also be used internally. For example, a firewall could be placed between a university's administrative system and the student side of its network. Firewalls employ one or more of four techniques: packet filter, application gateway, circuit-level gateway, and proxy server.[4]

A packet filter takes a look at the IP addresses of both the source and the target or destination of packets and, if appropriate, allows information to travel through specific holes or ports that have been opened on the firewall. Different Internet functions use different ports. FTP, for example, uses port 20; Web traffic (HTTP) travels through port 80. A packet filter on a firewall has a particular set of rules, its access control list, which governs what should be allowed through and what should be blocked. One rule, for example, might say that FTP traffic is permitted to be initiated from within the campus network (to go out) but not allowed to be initiated from off campus (to come in). By the way, networking types refer to the network space behind the firewall as the clean side and that on the other side (such as the Internet) as the dirty side.

Packet filters look only at the header of an information packet, but do no analysis of the content of that packet. Hackers can affix malicious data to a perfectly acceptable header and cause all sorts of damage. Yet the packet filter would let it through, because the packet on the surface appears legitimate.[5]

A firewall can employ an application gateway. This technique, used with an FTP server, for example, works well, but can slow things down.

A circuit-level gateway does its work when a connection is first established. After the gateway is convinced a connection is safe, it stops checking.[6]

The fourth possible technique used by a firewall is the proxy server. Proxy servers take a couple of extra steps beyond what a packet filter does. They actually look at the contents of information packets, again employing a set of rules. A packet that looks like an FTP session must, for example, contain the correct commands that you would expect to find in FTP.

Perhaps even more important, the proxy server functions as an intermediary between the requestor and the data source. The data from the source never travels directly to the end user, because the requesting client machine has set up the server as its proxy. The proxy server makes the information request on behalf of the requestor, retrieves the information and analyzes it, as described above. If everything checks out, the proxy server takes the valid data and inserts it into a new packet, which is sent to the requestor.[7]

Many college campuses use proxy servers for all Internet traffic, bypassing the proxies only for local Web addresses. Configuring a Web browser to use a proxy server is simple. On Internet Explorer 6, for example, one need only go into

Tools = > Internet Options = > Connections = > LAN Settings

and select "Use a proxy server for your LAN," then type in the address of that server.

Some proxy servers require this configuration; others, such as EZproxy, a product very popular with libraries, does not require configuration on the client end. It's all handled by the proxy server software itself.[8]

PROXY SERVERS AND REMOTE USER AUTHENTICATION

Some commercial databases require a user name and password to access them. At best, this is an awkward method for authentication. First, it is anything but transparent to the user. Second, it requires that someone maintain user names and passwords, disseminate the information to the users, reset passwords when the users forget them or mistype them and lock up accounts. This is an incredible hassle. An alternative would be to have a single user name and password, sharing it out to everyone, but this isn't particularly secure.

A more elegant approach is to use a machine's IP address to validate the user with databases to which an institution legally has access. Remember that a device connected to the Internet must have a unique IP address. Every organization, whether a company (.com), non-profit (.org), higher education institution (.edu), government agency (.gov) and so forth, gets assigned a block or blocks of IP addresses. The IP addresses for Swarthmore look much like each other, but very different from those at Pepperdine. Swarthmore can subscribe to a database then provide that database vendor with a list of valid IP addresses for its campus. The DB owner can set up its systems to recognize those addresses and let in PCs with IP addresses that are on the list.

Validating a user by means of IP addresses works great for on-campus computers, but by itself not for remote users. A user trying to access a database
from home could be connecting via almost any Internet Service Provider,
each of which has its own block of IP addresses. The Pepperdine student connecting through a RoadRunner cable modem gets a RoadRunner IP address,
which doesn't match the block of IP addresses for valid Pepperdine users. So
the student can't get in.

Proxy servers work wonderfully well for remote access. A user can configure her Web browser to use a campus proxy server, so that no matter what
ISP is used for Internet connectivity, Web queries will appear to come from
the proxy server, which has a valid campus IP address. With a product like
EZproxy, configuration isn't even necessary, because the server does it all.
The proxy server gains access and transparently passes information back and
forth between the user and the database. And she can do her research.

If these proxy servers are configured properly, they require the user first
to validate against a campus list of valid users. This list could come from
such sources as the campus network or the library's circulation database.
The library database is particularly handy, because it can also take advantage
of other features, such as the ability to block a user when s/he hasn't paid a
library fine, for example. Yet when proxy servers are not configured properly,
when user authentication does not occur, the opportunities for abuse are
enormous.

When JSTOR announced the security breach last December, its officials
blamed open proxy servers on college campuses. It should be noted that any
personal computer on a campus network can be set up as a Web server. For
example, Microsoft used to have a completely free product called Personal
Web Server software. It is also possible to find free proxy server software, as
I just did two minutes ago via a Google search. According to Kevin Guthrie,
president of JSTOR, "Anybody on a campus can set up a Web server and can
either accidentally or for some other reason open up some other proxies."[9]
The problem, says Guthrie, is that "People have figured this out. They understand this. So what they do is they go out and search for these open proxies."[10] If the computer is left on, and if a hacker can discover this machine,
he has an open door to whatever Web-enabled databases that machine can
access.

This is how a portion of JSTOR's collection of digital materials was stolen.
There are hundreds, perhaps thousands of open proxy servers on the nation's
campuses. In January, *Library Journal* reported that Melissa Belvadi, a systems and services librarian at Maryville University in St. Louis, wondered
how hard it would be to exploit this weakness. She searched Google for open
proxies and quickly uncovered a site listing a number of them. Using some
of the addresses from the list, she had no problem getting into databases
licensed by other schools, databases to which her own institution did not

have subscriptions.[11] I repeated her Google experiment and also found several lists of unsecured open proxies.

Open proxy servers are trouble. Aside from the illicit activity described above, they can be used for denial of service attacks. (A denial of service attack attempts to crash a network by overwhelming it with useless traffic.[12]) Open proxies can also be used to aid with spam mailings.

WHAT CAN BE DONE

There are several strategies for addressing the problem of open proxy servers and the need for secure and effective authentication.

1. Return to the old days of requiring a user name and password for access to each database. I don't think anyone wants to do that.

2. Develop mechanisms for identifying open proxy servers on campuses and shut them down.

3. Configure the main campus firewall correctly so that it won't allow off-campus access to any open proxy servers that might exist on campus.

4. Configure all institutional computers to travel through a main campus proxy server for all Web traffic. There are a couple of problems with this approach. It puts a burden on one server and creates a single failure point, that is, if the proxy service stops or if the server crashes, all Internet connectivity stops cold.

5. Don't use proxy services for remote access to databases, but instead employ something like a virtual private network (VPN). Many schools, such as the University of Pittsburgh, are employing VPNs to provide a more secure off-site connection to the campus network. A virtual private network travels over the Internet, authenticates the user, and encrypts data. The remote machine becomes part of the network, gets assigned a campus IP address and has direct access to whatever resources a campus machine does, including library databases. In this scenario, there is no need for a proxy server, because the client already has a valid IP address. However, VPNs require installation of software on the client machine at home, which puts a support burden on campus IT. In addition, VPN encryption can slow the performance of the connection.[13] Finally, VPNs have their own security limitations.

6. Investigate other alternatives. The Shibboleth Project, for example, is developing architecture for sharing information resources among colleges and universities with the appropriate access controls. This is a more complicated security environment, involving personal attributes of users in higher education, trust relationships among campuses/networks, and so forth.[14]

Something needs to change though. As JSTOR says on its Web site, "as long as IP authentication remains a primary authorization mechanism for resources, and as long as open proxy servers continue to proliferate, no technical solution can be 100% effective."[15] In the meantime, JSTOR intends to take action against any open proxies it identifies that are trying to access its resources. Other publishers, if they feel similarly threatened, are likely to follow suit. Responses would certainly include blocking access from unauthorized proxies, but other responses could be legal in nature.

DANGERS ABOUND

Cybertheft is not new, though it is happening with increasing frequency and potentially devastating consequences. In March, someone hacked into systems at the University of Texas at Austin and stole the names and social security numbers of 52,000 individuals.[16] Fortunately, the individual was caught, apparently before he'd used the information to ill effect. I say fortunately, because with this kind of data, a good cyberthief could tap into financial accounts, stealing millions of dollars. In an age where information and money are electronic, the risks are very high.

Academic librarians are proponents of broad access to information, anytime and anyplace, for their user communities. Whether a current student or faculty member is on campus or in a cyber cafe in Paris should be irrelevant. Librarians strive to provide transparent systems, with a minimal amount of barriers between the user and the information she or he is seeking. Librarians also want to ensure user privacy and academic freedom. These are all laudable values.

But the publishing community has legitimate concerns as well. It took a lot to convince journal and index publishers to share their information resources electronically. A story like JSTOR's should be as scary to us as it is to these publishers, for if we don't provide a secure computing environment in which researchers can use the publishers' assets, those publishers may understandably want to pull back from the open access they have provided in the past. That would be a tragedy for scholarship inquiry. To protect our interests, we must protect theirs.

NOTES

1. "Open Proxy Servers: Gateways to Unauthorized Use of Licensed Resources." 2002. *JSTOR NEWS* 6 (December). http://www.jstor.org/news/2002.12/open-proxy.html.

2. Dan Carnevale. 2003. "Security Lapses Permit Theft from Database of Scholarly Journals." *The Chronicle of Higher Education* (January): A29.

3. Ibid.

4. www.webopedia.com/TERM/f/firewall.html.

5. Terry William Ogletree. 2001. "The First Line of Defense." *PC Magazine* (June): 92.

6. www.webopedia.com/TERM/f/firewall.html.

7. Ogletree, op. cit.

8. Bertrand Gordon. 2002. "Providing Access to Remote Patrons Can Be EZ," *Feliciter*: 135.

9. Carnevale, op. cit.

10. Ibid.

11. "Open Proxy Servers Victimize JSTOR," *Library Journal* (January 2003): 20.

12. http://www.webopedia.com/TERM/D/DoS_attack.html.

13. Florence Olsen. 2001. "Colleges Offer New Connections to Networks from Off Campus," *The Chronicle of Higher Education* 47 (August): A31.

14. http://shibboleth.internet2.edu.

15. http://www.jstore.org/about/openproxies.html.

16. Vincent Kiernan. 2003. "U. of Texas Student Is Charged in Theft of Social Security Numbers," *The Chronicle of Higher Education*. 49 (March): A31.

4

OPENURL BASICS

Walt Crawford

OpenURL is a leveraging and amplifying technology. Relatively small and simple by itself, it improves a library's existing resources by allowing them to work better together. The basics of OpenURL are fairly straightforward but allow for a surprising variety of implementations. After noting the elements that make up OpenURL and the process involved in an OpenURL transaction, I will discuss some of the variations I have encountered in current link-resolver configurations, systems that link bibliographic citations to available source materials.

One caveat: I have used more than a hundred different OpenURL resolvers in conjunction with RLG's Eureka as an OpenURL source, but I have never actually configured or implemented an OpenURL resolver. I understand the principles, but not necessarily the down-and-dirty details of rule or template building and knowledge-base maintenance.

WHAT IT IS, HOW IT WORKS[1]

An OpenURL transaction requires that an OpenURL source generate an OpenURL message (usually because a user clicks on an OpenURL trigger) and send it to an OpenURL resolver identified by an OpenURL base address. The resolver processes the message using a knowledge base and rule sets and generates some number of OpenURL services, some of which use OpenURL targets.

Now, let us look at each of these elements in turn, starting with the missing piece, the OpenURL protocol itself. The OpenURL metadata protocol defines a set of elements to identify a bibliographic item (and a few other things) and a syntax to put those elements together and do something with them. OpenURL 0.1 provides for a base address (nothing more than a regular URL, pointing to a piece of software somewhere) and such items as author's last name, author's first name or initial, title of an article, title of a journal or book, ISSN or ISBN, and date, volume, issue, and pages of a journal (or book) in which an article (or chapter) resides. It also provides ways to identify who is creating the information.

In order for a library or consortium to use OpenURL, it must buy, build, or subscribe to an OpenURL resolver (sometimes known as a link resolver), and buy, build, or edit the knowledge base and rule set that will support the library or consortium.

The knowledge base typically includes all serials known to the library or its OpenURL vendor (or a third party), including titles, ISSNs, and whether (and how) the library or consortium can provide full text, abstracts, or other information on articles within each serial. The latter portion can appear multiply—one serial may be available through half a dozen different full-text sources—and includes date ranges, restrictions ("all volumes since 1980, but not including the last five years"), and access methodology (both the technical details and whether full text within a given resource can be addressed directly at the article level, only at the issue level, only at the journal level, or—in at least one well-known case—only at the front door to the entire full-text service).

The rule set (or decision set) is used to determine what OpenURL services to offer and in what order, based on the metadata contained within the OpenURL message and what's in the knowledge base. The rule set may also include special provisions for some OpenURL sources (special parsing of metadata because of known issues, for example). So, for example, if a given periodical for a given year is available from several sources, the rule set should determine which source to list first. If a search is offered against a local or a union catalog, the rule set should determine what *kind* of search to do (and whether to offer choices to the user.) The decision set should also include provisions for incomplete OpenURL transactions (either because of faulty OpenURL sources or because the databases underlying the sources do not have full information) and sets of services to offer when neither full text nor print holdings are available (e.g., populating an interlibrary loan [ILL] request, searching open-archive harvesters, searching the title in Google or AllTheWeb or, for a book, searching either the ISBN or the author's name in a commercial service).

The library or consortium must activate OpenURL with each desired OpenURL source, directly or indirectly, which involves providing the OpenURL base address (the Internet location at which the resolver is to be found, which may be at the library or hosted by a vendor) and, usually, providing another address for the OpenURL trigger image, although most

OpenURL sources should provide a default trigger as well. (RLG's Eureka uses "Availability" as a default.)

Step by Step

Here's what happens when a library user searching a database wants more information about a particular article, book chapter, journal, or book:

1. The user clicks on the OpenURL trigger, which should appear above, next to, or beneath each record.

2. The database provider, an OpenURL source, generates an OpenURL message: An address consisting of the OpenURL base address for the library or consortium and the OpenURL metadata for the desired item. The source then opens a new browser window with that transaction as an address. The OpenURL source's role in the transaction is now complete. (Note that metasearch engines may also act as OpenURL sources, even for databases that are not themselves OpenURL sources.)

3. The OpenURL resolver then processes the OpenURL message against its rule set and knowledge base. Depending on the decision set and resolver design, the resolver may carry out some other operations in advance—for example, doing a catalog search automatically.

4. The OpenURL resolver populates the browser window with some set of OpenURL services (or a message that no services are available for the item), in an order determined by the decision set. The resolver also, in most cases, provides a page heading identifying the institution or consortium and a redisplay of the requested item. In cases where presearching is done, some resolvers can show the results of the catalog search within the resolver window. Services appear as live links—to full-text sources, to online catalog searches, to Google, to ILL forms.

5. The user selects an OpenURL service, which will either replace the resolver window or open another window. Unless the user goes back for a different service, that completes the OpenURL transaction. With luck, the user now has full text for an article (or book, in a few thousand cases), identification of print holdings, or some other satisfactory service.

What about OpenURL targets? A target is really anything that an OpenURL resolver can point to—and there's no need for the target to know anything about OpenURL. For example, many databases understand Z39.50 search-and-retrieval syntax and make appropriate targets without OpenURL awareness. Some target resources may support OpenURL syntax directly.

The key element, the OpenURL resolver, may be homegrown (as some of the best are), purchased from among 10 or more vendors, or used on a subscription basis with the actual resolver running at the vendor's site. The crucial knowledge base may come from the same vendor or some other source; "jake" is the best-known open source knowledge base. Every knowledge base requires local customization, since no library's set of resources perfectly matches those of any other library. Put that together and it means better use of a library's resources. Just click and see what is available.

OpenURL 1.0, which should soon be approved as a National Information Standards Organization (NISO) standard, adds more formality and a whole new set of possibilities—and that's another story, one not suitable for this chapter.

Details of an OpenURL Message

I'll discuss OpenURL 0.1 because it has less administrative overhead than OpenURL 1.0 and appears simpler, although the basic set of elements is identical (except for slight syntax variations) in both versions.

An OpenURL message is a URL transmitted either as an HTTP GET or HTTP POST statement. It begins with the URL for the OpenURL resolver, which is followed by metadata consisting of label-element pairs. Most label-element pairs used in OpenURL transactions are defined in the OpenURL 0.1 specification, but there's a private area that allows for extended elements—assuming that the resolver and OpenURL source agree on the set and meaning of those extended elements.

Most if not all elements are optional; none can occur more than once within a transaction (in OpenURL 0.1). The appearance of each element is simply "label = value," with ampersands separating label-element pairs—but most nonalphabetic characters within values must be encoded as hexadecimal values for transmission, which makes OpenURL messages hard to read by humans.

Here's a record from RLG's Anthropology *Plus* database displayed in Eureka's Brief format:

Janetski, Joel C.

Distinctive bone disks from Utah Valley: evidence of Basketmaker connections in North Central Utah.

In: Kiva Vol. 68, no. 4 (2003), p. 305–22, ISSN 0023–1940.

Here's that record as an encoded OpenURL:

```
http://olinks.ohiolink.edu/olinks.php?sid%3ERLG%3AANT%3Cgenre%3Ear
ticle%3Caulast%3EJanetski%3Caufirst%3EJoel%3Cauinit%3EC.%3Cissn%3E00
23–1940%3Ctitle%3EKiva%3Catitle%3EDistinctive%20bone%20disks%20from
%20Utah%20Valley%3A%20evidence%20of%20Basketmaker%20connections%2
0in%20North%20Central%20Utah%3Cvolume%3E68%3Cissue%3E4%3Cspage%
3E305%3Cepage%3E22%3Cpages%3E305–22%3Cdate%3E2003%3Cpid%3Eid
%3EXRAI03M1011YRAW6635%3Aaloc%3EVol.%2068%2C%20no.%204%20%
262003%27%2C%20p.%20305–22%2C
```

Here's the same OpenURL without the encoding, making it *slightly* more readable:

---

http://olinks.ohiolink.edu/olinks.php?sid = RLG:ANT&genre = article&aulast = Janetski&aufirst = Joel&auinit = C.&issn = 0023–1940&title = Kiva&atitle = Distinctive bone disks from Utah Valley: evidence of Basketmaker connections in North Central Utah&volume = 68&issue = 4&spage = 305&epage = 22&pages = 305–22&date = 2003&pid = id = XRAI03M1011YRAW6635:aloc = Vol. 68, no. 4 (2003), p. 305–22

Let's step through each of those elements, fairly typical of an OpenURL 0.1 transaction. There could be fewer, more, or in some cases slightly different elements, but this set is typical except for the final section.

- **http://olinks.ohiolink.edu/olinks.php:** The BaseURL for OhioLINK's resolver.
- **sid = RLG:ANT:** Source ID, identifying the OpenURL source (RLG) and the specific database (ANT, RLG's standard abbreviation for Anthropology *Plus*).
- **genre = article:** Genre identification, so the resolver knows whether it is dealing with an article, a chapter in a book ("bookitem"), a journal, or a book.
- **aulast = Janetski:** Last name of the first author of the article.
- **aufirst = Joel:** First name of the first author of the article.
- **auinit = C.:** Middle initial of the first author.
- **issn = 0023–1940:** ISSN for the journal.
- **title = Kiva:** Title of the journal (or book), not the article.
- **atitle = Distinctive bone disks from Utah Valley: evidence of Basketmaker connections in North Central Utah:** Title of the article or chapter.
- **volume = 68:** Volume in which the article appears.
- **issue = 4:** Issue in which the article appears.
- **spage = 305:** Starting page for the article—redundant information in most cases (see "pages") added because some resolvers cannot parse the "pages" element, and the starting page is useful for direct linking to a full-text article.
- **epage = 22:** Ending page for the article—but note that this is erroneous, as a consequence of normal "pages" entry rules and machine parsing. Fortunately, it is also redundant.
- **pages = 305–22:** Page range for the article, which most resolvers can use to determine starting page.
- **date = 2003:** Year of publication.
- **pid = id = XRAI03M1011YRAW6635:** The first element in the private area of an OpenURL transaction (identified by "pid"), in this case the record ID for the source record—useful if a resolver chooses to get further information using Z39.50 or other retrieval technique.
- **aloc = Vol. 68, no. 4 (2003), p. 305–22:** A temporary oddity within Eureka OpenURLs. In designing Eureka's implementation, I looked at cases (mostly in a

few specialized databases) where we could not reliably parse out the volume, issue, page, and date information from the subfield containing all this information (773 subfield g, for MARC junkies). The code "aloc" (article location), the full contents of 773$g, was added in the hope that some resolvers might be able to do a better job of parsing than Eureka does. To the best of my knowledge, has never been used (and we continue to improve Eureka's parsing), and will probably be eliminated after polling our OpenURL users.

VARIATIONS ON A THEME

For most resolvers and most uses, the first service you hope to see is full-text availability from one or more sources—JSTOR, Highwire, LexisNexis, EBSCO Expanded Academic, ScienceDirect, direct available for OA publishers, what have you. Everything else is secondary. As I have tested resolvers, one thing that has impressed me is the extent to which OpenURL pulls together disparate resources. I use two test searches in Anthropology *Plus* and two more in each of the anthropology databases that make up that service; I check the first 25 results for each search.

Every institution with decent full-text resources winds up showing more than one full-text resource within a 25-record result set. The number of resources involved can be astonishingly large.

For example, the first 25 records for one keyword search, checked against the resources of one Association of Research Libraries (ARL) library, yielded full text from the following sources: Free e-journals, Catchword, Metapress, Swetsnet, Academic Search Premier, EBSCO Health Source Nursing, Ingenta, Synergy, LexisNexis, OCLC Contemporary Women's Issues, Cambridge University Press, Factiva, Proquest ABI/Inform, OCLC Wilson Select Plus, and Project Muse—as well as articles represented in print holdings but not available in full text. That's 16 different sources in one 25-record result set.

I will assert that no student or faculty member would *ever* search 16 different resources—and if they did (using metasearch techniques), the focused results from a professionally prepared index would be muddied by other results because of homonyms from fields other than anthropology.

That is the basic power. What of the variations and choices?

Full-Text Variations

The easiest situation is when an OpenURL points to a journal for which a library has full-text access through one and only one source, and when that source allows links at the article level. The resolver shows that link—or, possibly, authenticates the user and goes *directly* to the full-text display.

But it is not always that easy. Frequently, the journal will be available through several sources. Which source should appear first (knowing that most users will click on that one)? How many sources should appear (I have seen as many as eight sources for a single journal)? What should appear for each source? That is not a singular issue. For example:

- Some institutions use text reminding the user that the library or consortium is making the full-text version possible; e.g. "Neverland University Library makes this article available through Alltext." Most don't.
- Different institutions use different names for the same full-text aggregation—e.g., either "Elsevier" or "ScienceDirect" or both.
- Some (but not all) configurations show the year/volume/issue/page values as a row of labels and prefilled entry boxes below each full-text source—or show that information only when the source can be reached at that level.
- Some institutions offer hints for dealing with full-text resources that do not offer direct article linking; those hints usually appear below the source name, either in addition to or in place of year/volume/issue/page values.

There is no right or wrong here; rather, there's a set of decisions to make, depending on the flexibility offered in your resolver.

Presearching the Catalog

I have seen at least two ways to integrate local print holdings into the resolver. Some institutions populate the resolver's knowledge base with print holdings, so that *known* local holdings show up along with full-text offerings in the resolver window. Others presearch the local catalog, a union catalog, or both—and that presearching can be done for books as well as journals and articles.

Why do a presearch? For some resolvers, it is because you can bring back the print holdings and display them as part of the resolver window, although most configurations require the user to click on the local catalog link to repeat the search. In that case, the presearch serves to modify or eliminate the local catalog link. So, for example, if print holdings do appear, the link might say "Check availability at Neverland University library," where if an ISSN search fails, it might say "Neverland University library may hold this item," with the link leading to a title search.

Some institutions go further: If the ISSN search fails, there is no link to the local catalog at all. These configurations are generally those that stop at standard numbers, not offering title or author-title searches for books or journals/articles. (Some resolver configurations *only* handle journals, but that restriction is declining.)

Searching Catalogs

Assuming a resolver offers catalog searches at all (and some do not), there are many valid variations in that common theme:

- Some resolvers offer consortial and union catalog searches first, particularly when the union catalog includes all local holdings. Others go first to the campus catalog—and may or may not offer union catalogs.

- Some resolvers offer catalog searches beyond the local and direct union catalog, reaching out to a broader range of catalogs, possibly including the RLG Union Catalog and WorldCat.

- Should book searches use ISBN? That would seem like an obvious choice, but some very high quality resolvers use title instead, so that the user is offered alternate editions of the book in question. Some resolvers offer both ISBN and title searches, just as some resolvers allow for both ISSN and journal title searches.

- If an online catalog allows for title browses (where the desired title appears as the second or third item in a list, or the place where the title *would* be is in that position), title searches can be more fulfilling. Frequently, the form of the title in the source database will not precisely match the form of the title in the target catalog. That is true for both journals and books.

- For that matter, title phrase searching is not the only way to do a title search. Some resolvers use title word searches instead. Some use keyword searches. And some resolvers use authors along with titles, either when titles are short or in other innovative ways. (One resolver does an author search and uses the title as a limit, defaulting to the author result set if the title is not found.)

Other Service Possibilities

Most resolver configurations offer a small set of services. Most commonly, the only extra besides full-text and catalog searching is an ILL form—and some resolvers *only* offer the ILL form if there is no full text and no indication of local print holdings. That makes some sense, given findings that many ILL requests are for items already available locally.

I have seen other possibilities that, sometimes in resolvers with more than a dozen service options:

- Searches against indexes that harvest OAI-compliant (open access) repositories, such as University of Michigan's OAIster. That index now includes more than three million articles; that can make it a serious source of free access to journal articles where a library does not license full text of the journal. Such searches will typically be for the article title but could also be for articles by the author.

- Searches against the open Web, via either Google or some other search engine. Such searches could use article or book title, journal title or ISSN, author name, ISBN, or other possibilities. Article/book title is probably most common.

- Article/journal services other than full text, such as article abstracts, tables of contents, and information from Ulrich's or Web of Science.

- Book services, including book reviews from various sources and possibly online buying possibilities.

- Formatted bibliographic citations based on the OpenURL metadata.

Design Decisions

Design decisions come in three general areas. First, should the trigger for OpenURL be the OpenURL source's default ("Availability" for Eureka), the OpenURL resolver vendor's default (usually the vendor logo), or a campus-specific image? If it is campus specific, should it be meaningful text, and, if so, what is the best text to use?

Second, should the resolver window itself be the vendor's default design, or should it be customized for the library? I have never been thrilled with the gray-green background color used in many resolver windows, and I am pleased to see that it is being replaced by a simple white background in more and more cases. Similarly, most recent resolver configurations feature the campus or consortium name or logo. Most resolver windows place a brief citation (repeating the OpenURL information) below that logo, but some resolvers are silent as to the source. Typographic and other decisions enter into this area.

Third, how should service offerings work? In some cases, the name of the target service is a hotlink. In others, the full description—prefatory text and target name—serves as a hotlink. And there are cases where only a small logo to the left of each service description is live. There are other design decisions, to be sure, including the size of the browser window when a catalog search is initiated. (Typically, the OpenURL source determines the size of the resolver window.)

NEW POSSIBILITIES IN OPENURL 1.0

OpenURL 0.1 emerged from the pioneering work of Herbert Van de Sompel and other creators of SFX. The "0.1" version number has been added as OpenURL approaches approval as a formal NISO standard, Z39.88, which would be called OpenURL 1.0.

Z39.88 strengthens OpenURL by making it an open standard that does not in any way rely on a single company. Ex Libris' product, SFX, has avoided the temptation to change the definition of OpenURL to give SFX an advantage over other resolvers, but the best way to assure even-handedness in the long run is standardization. Because Z39.88 is (or will be) a NISO standard, the standards documents will be freely available for downloading—a NISO characteristic that is not true of many other ANSI and ISO standards organization.

Z39.88 also adds a range of new possibilities and is fundamentally open ended to allow for other new possibilities. Additionally, the "info:uri" schema defined to register certain numbering and identification schemes without complex management overhead will encourage new uses and users.

Some characteristics of Z39.88, in brief:

- It is possible to send OpenURL data by reference (e.g., "here is the ID: you pick it up") rather than directly, although that substantially increases the overhead of the service.

- It is possible to use XML with its enormous overhead in lieu of the brief OpenURL Key/Encoded-Value (KEV) notation. Indeed, given the info: registry for metadata formats, you could even register other possible formats.
- OpenURL 0.1 messages consist of three entities: the resolver (BaseURL), the referrer (the database or source that created the message), and the referent (the resource of interest). OpenURL 1.0 adds three new optional entities: the referring entity (e.g., an article that includes a reference that becomes the referent), the requester (a person or agency requesting specific services related to the referent), and the service type (the service requested by the requester).
- The new optional entities add to the potential complexity of OpenURL 1.0, but also allow for a range of additional services.

If there is a downside to Z39.88 as compared to OpenURL 0.1, it is indicated in that last bullet point: complexity. The documents defining Z39.88 are several times as long as the primary document for OpenURL 0.1 and much more difficult to understand. There will be briefer documents that set out subset requirements for OpenURL 1.0, but initially it appears to be a more difficult protocol to implement. Unless an agency chooses to support the optional new entities, that is mostly appearance. In the long run, with supporting documents, Z39.88 (OpenURL 1.0) should increase the power and flexibility of an already powerful, flexible standard.

WHY OPENURL MATTERS

First and most important, OpenURL leverages your existing resources by connecting indexes with full text and your catalog—getting students and faculty from the article they are interested in to your full-text and print resources in a single step. OpenURL also makes it easy for people to move from one full-text resource to a related one, using digital object identifiers (DOI) or other schemes to link a reference in one paper to the referenced paper. Good OpenURL parsing might even create such a link without special procedures.

OpenURL can make open access and institutionally archived papers more visible and more valuable, as campuses add OAIster and other harvester searches to their resolvers. Your users may be able to view papers in journals that you do not have in full text, if the articles are available elsewhere.

OpenURL makes related services easier. If you do not have the resource at all, OpenURL can populate your ILL request with bibliographic information. A resolver may also offer searches of the open Web for more information on the title or the author.

OpenURL is not rocket science. A number of institutions have developed their own resolvers. The most difficult part of most resolvers is not the resolver at all: it is the knowledge base. OpenURL resolvers can make use of existing standards as well; for example, by using Z39.50 to search local catalogs.

OpenURL does not have many weaknesses, but there are a few. First, some source data is inherently incomplete. There are no ISSNs for nineteenth-century periodicals, for example, and no ISBNs for early books. Second, neither OpenURL 0.1 nor 1.0 will really handle articles from the many older (and ceased) periodicals cataloged with corporate authors, since there is no place to put the author of the journal. Currently, OpenURL does not handle the case where the author or editor of a book is different than the author of the desired chapter and the author's name is essential to identify the book, although that weakness may be resolved.

Then there are the usual fallibilities. Some OpenURL sources do not parse source data appropriately, sending incomplete or erroneous OpenURLs. Some resolvers do not handle exceptional cases very well. *Many* possible targets do not understand Z39.50 or cannot begin a session with a search already in place. Some full-text aggregations do not allow direct entry to the article, and some do not even provide direct access to the journal or year.

OpenURL works. It is a prime example of a small development with big impact.

NOTE

1. This section, up to "Step by Step," originally appeared in *Cites & Insights: Crawford at Large* 4, no. 2 (Midwinter 2004). That issue is available at http://cites.boisestate.edu/civ4i2.pdf.

FURTHER READING

Beit-Arie, Oren, Blake, Miriam, Caplan, Priscilla, Flecker, Dale, Ingoldsby, Tim, Lannom, Laurence W., Mischo, William H., Pentz, Edward, Rogers, Sally, and Van de Sompel, Herbert. (2001). Linking to the appropriate copy: report of a DOI-based prototype. *D-Lib Magazine, 7* (September).

Caplan, Priscilla, and Arms, William Y. (1999). Reference linking for journal articles. *D-Lib Magazine* 5 (July/August).

Cook, Anita, and Dowling, Thomas. (2003). Linking from index to primary source: the OhioLINK model. *The Journal of Academic Librarianship, 29*(5), 320–326.

Crawford, Walt. (2004, February). The Crawford files: OpenURL meets open access. *American Libraries, 35,* 52.

Crawford, Walt. (2002, August). The Crawford files: OpenURL: Standards can be fun! *American Libraries, 33,* 99.

Cummings, Joel, and Johnson, Ryan. (2003). "The use and usability of SFX: Context-sensitive reference linking." *Library Hi Tech, 21*(1), 70–84.

Gerrity, Bob, Lyman, Theresa, and Tallent, Ed. (2002). "Blurring services and resources: Boston College's implementation of MetaLib and SFX." *Reference Services Review, 30*(3), 229–241.

Hellman, Eric. (2003). OpenURL: Making the link to libraries. *Learned Publishing, 16*(3), 177–181.

Hendricks, Arthur. (2003). The Development of the NISO Committee AX's OpenURL Standard. *Information Technology and Libraries, 22*(3), 129–133.

Lewis, Nicholas. (2003). 'I want it all and I want it now!' Managing expectations with MetaLib and SFX at the University of East Anglia. *Serials, 16*(1), 89–95.

Needleman, Mark H. (2002). The OpenURL: An emerging standard for linking. *Serials Review, 28*(1), 74–76.

Powell, Andy. (2001, June). "OpenResolver: A simple OpenURL resolver." *Ariadne, 28.*

Powell, Andy, and Apps, Ann. (2001, March). Metadata (1): Encoding OpenURLs in DC metadata. *Ariadne, 27.*

RLG Focus, 56 (2002, June). Includes several case studies of OpenURL implementation.

Soderdahl, Paul A. (2003). Implementing the SFX Link Server at the University of Iowa. *Information Technology and Libraries, 22*(3), 117–119.

Stern, David. (2001, March/April). Automating enhanced discovery and delivery: The OpenURL possibilities. *Online, 25*(2), 42–47.

Van de Sompel, Herbert, and Beit-Arie, Oren. (2001, July/August). Generalizing the OpenURL framework beyond references to scholarly works: The Bison-Futé model. *D-Lib Magazine, 7.*

Van de Sompel, Herbert, and Beit-Arie, Oren. (2001, March). Open linking in the scholarly information environment using the OpenURL framework. *D-Lib Magazine, 7.*

Walker, Jenny. (2002).CrossRef and SFX: Complementary linking services for libraries. *New Library World, 103*(3), 83–89.

Walker, Jenny. (2001). Open linking for libraries: The OpenURL framework. *New Library World, 102*(4/5), 127–133.

Walker, Jenny. (2001, October). What Is SFX? *Learned Publishing, 14,* 296–298.

5

<hr>

RADIO FREQUENCY
IDENTIFICATION (RFID)

Eric H. Schnell

Radio Frequency Identification (RFID) is a material-identification system that is a combination of radio frequency and microchip technologies. Unlike traditional bar codes, which require strict line-of-sight access in order to be read, RFID is a noncontact, non-line-of-sight technology. The use of radio waves allows that the material-identification tag can be placed anywhere on an item and can even be covered over with a label. The use of microchip technology allows several tags to be read quickly at one time and from any orientation. In libraries, RFID technology can speed up item checkout, check-in, inventory, and shelving activities and simplify scanning functions for staff and patrons. It can provide both inventory-related and theft-deterrence functions, which save the time and resources of installing separate systems for each of these functions. RFID scanners can be built into book-return units and automatically check in materials as they are dropped. Customer and collection records can be automatically updated in real time.

RFID technology was originally developed during World War II as a way to distinguish between friendly and enemy aircraft. It was not until the 1970s that the technology was revived by the U.S. government to track livestock and for security and safety surrounding the use of nuclear materials. Soon after, the technology was transferred from government labs to the public sector. Many applications of RFID technology have since made their way into our daily lives. For example, Exxon Mobil's Speedpass allows customers to pay for gas or groceries. The E-ZPass electronic toll collection (ETC) consortium stores account information on an RFID tag installed in a vehicle and is read by a receiving antenna at the toll plaza. The toll is electronically deducted from a prepaid toll account. Many vehicles have an RFID-based remote keyless entry system. Several major retailers, including Wal-Mart, and the U.S. military require their largest suppliers to put RFID tags on their products.

A basic RFID system consists of three components: the tag contains a microchip that stores unique identifier and other information, the reader extracts the information on the tag, and an antenna acts as a conduit between the tag and the reader by emitting radio signals that excite the microchip, allowing the stored information to be read. A library-oriented RFID system may also include the following components:

- *Circulation stations.* Check out materials while updating the customer and collection records.
- *Staff processing stations.* Used to process new materials and write data to the RFID tag while updating the collection record.
- *Shelf-management readers.* Hand-held "wands" that collect inventory data as well as search for items for retrieval or weeding out.
- *Theft-deterrence gates.* Check the security status of materials as customers exit, and sound an alarm when items are not checked out.
- *Self-checkout stations.* Accept a customer identification card and check out the materials, deactivate the security bit, and print a receipt.
- *Return drops.* Have built-in scanners that automatically check in materials and update the customer and collection records.
- *Sorting stations.* When combined with a return drop, these can automatically sort items for shelving.

THE RFID TAG

The key component of an RFID system is the tag, which consists of a memory chip and an antenna. RFID tags are paper thin, wireless, and both readable and writeable. When passed near a reading station, a radio field charges the chip contained in the tag and allows it to transmit its data. RFID tags hold several advantages over bar codes:

- Line of sight is not required to read the RFID tag, and it does not need to be visible or properly aligned to be read successfully.
- RFID tags can be applied anywhere on materials.
- Several tags can be read at one time, so a small stack of materials can be read at once.
- RFID tags are more tamper resistant than bar codes.
- Antitheft capabilities can be built into the tag, providing both material identification and security.

RFID vendors utilize different tag designs and frequencies for their systems, each of which has different characteristics that make them more useful in certain applications. The technology used in library applications is considered to be passive, meaning the tags have no batteries. Instead, the tags draw power from the readers, which send out electromagnetic waves that create a current in the tag's antenna. Different RFID systems will also use different radio-frequency bands. Low-frequency tags that use less power and are better able to penetrate nonmetallic substances are cheaper than ultra-high-frequency (UHF) tags. UHF frequencies typically offer better range and can transfer data faster but use more power and are less likely to pass through materials. Library systems will generally utilize the short-range low-frequency technology.

Vendors have the ability to tightly control the formatting of the data on RFID tags, but some are more open about the format used. Some solutions only permit the unique bar code number and the security bit on the RFID tag, while others allow the library to add data such as the title and call number. The former must access the item record on the integrated library system (ILS) to get the information on the material, while the latter reads the information directly from the tag.

LIBRARY APPLICATIONS FOR RFID

New technologies have always been of interest for libraries, both for the potential of increasing the quality of service and for improving efficiency of operations. As libraries of all kinds face economic hardships, new technologies can offer potential cost savings in the operation and management of resources. RFID technology provides libraries with new and valuable productivity gains while enhancing customer services.

RFID technology can increase the speed and ergonomics of item processing in a library. It can improve the management of the collection, since the built-in memory can record information such as the location of the book in the library and statistics about usage. RFID tags can be read quickly and regardless of tag orientation or position, allowing for the implementation of reliable sorting systems. RFID systems update the library database in real time and supply more accurate information about availability of materials. Finally, RFID can reduce theft by integrating the antitheft function at all stages of the life of an item.

Resource Management

It is not uncommon for over half of a library's fiscal resources to be set aside for materials. Significant resources are also used in the management of those materials, as reflected by the fact that the departments with the largest staff in almost every full-service library are circulation and technical services. While consortium and bulk purchases of materials can help reduce acquisition costs, significant time and energy is spent by library staff executing very detailed process flow charts to deal with acquiring, cataloging, shelving, checking out, checking in, inventorying, and reshelving physical materials. Libraries are often forced to increase productivity with fewer employees, resulting in smaller staffs that require strategies designed to streamline material handling time. Significant human and fiscal resources more often are being reallocated to manage electronic collections. These facts lead to challenges associated with the management of physical materials, such as books, bound journals, and nonprint materials. Therefore, methods or technologies that allow staff to be more efficient, such as RFID, are certainly worth investigating.

Stack maintenance and inventory control are also time-consuming challenges for libraries and librarians. While wireless devices have helped to computerize these processes, they are still primarily hands-on tasks that utilize significant human resources. As a result, many libraries do not have accurate organization or inventories of their collections. A primary benefit of deploying RFID and its associated systems is that they help to simplify these tasks. A key component of a library RFID system is the shelf reader, a relatively lightweight hand-held unit that can scan materials on their shelves without tipping them out or removing them. The shelf reader can read up to 20 tags per second, making it possible to inventory a shelf in just a few seconds. To inventory the collection, the reader is moved past the book spines and information on the tags is stored in the portable unit. The unit is then attached to the ILS via a hardwired connection to either the circulation or staff processing workstations. Records can be downloaded into the reader to search for specific materials or to identify missing and misshelved items at the same time the inventory is being performed. By using wireless technology along with the shelf reader, it is possible not only to update the inventory but to identify in real time items that are out of proper order.

Circulation of Materials

Checking materials out and back in is another labor-intensive library process. Traditional bar codes require line of sight in order to be read, which may require reorienting materials in order to locate the bar codes prior to scanning. An RFID circulation station can help reduce time spent processing materials, since bar codes do not have to be located or materials reoriented before scanning. This time savings is further enhanced by the fact that several RFID tags can be scanned at the same time, allowing a small stack of materials to be scanned simultaneously.

Self-checkout aisles have become very popular in many retail stores. These aisles not only reduce the time a customer stands in line, they reduce staff workload. Library self-checkout stations have gained in popularity because of the time savings for circulation staff. Unlike the self-checkout stations in retail stores, a library self-checkout station designed for an RFID system has an antenna that reads the tag, updates the item record in the ILS, associates the item with the customer, and potentially update the security status simultaneously. The benefits of not having to locate the bar codes or reorient materials, and the ability to scan multiple items at once are extended to the customer. If the library also employs RFID-enabled customer cards, the identification of the customer can also be read by the self-checkout reader and further reduce the customer transaction time.

An RFID-enabled self-return drop can update customer and item records instantaneously while alerting library staff when reserve items are returned. Return drops that include a sorting station can check an item in, update the customer record and the security status, and then presort materials into bins. The sorter can be customized to categorize the materials in any order (e.g., reserve, reference, stacks) in order to speed reshelving.

Security

Bar codes do not prevent materials from being lost or stolen. To reduce the chance of theft, libraries traditionally have employed a host of measures, including metallic strips placed in materials and sensor gates that detect them. This relatively low-tech solution has served libraries well but requires staff time to place strips on the materials and to deactivate the strip at checkout and reactivate it at check-in. Most RFID solutions utilize tags which include a built-in security feature that can be more reliable than electromagnetic solutions. The security feature on each tag is checked as a customer passes through the security gate and sounds an alarm if the feature is not deactivated. The use of radio-frequency technology means that materials held overhead or kicked around a gate can also be captured. If materials are taken past the gates, and are not intercepted by staff, the library would at least know which items had been taken.

RFID systems that utilize the security feature allow libraries to eliminate the need to purchase and process materials using other theft-detection systems. A properly configured RFID security system also results in fewer false alarms than older technologies. RFID systems that do not use the security feature built into the tag must query the ILS to check security status before the customer walks through the gates. These systems could result in a queue that may allow customers to leave the library with materials that are not checked out to them.

It is possible to compromise an RFID system by wrapping library materials that have tags in two to three layers of ordinary household foil to block the radio signal. An RFID system can also be compromised by placing two items against one another so that one tag overlays another, which may cancel out the signals. Compromising an RFID system in either manner does require knowledge of the technology and careful alignment of the materials.

Cost

The major disadvantage of being an early adopter of any technology is cost, as is the case with RFID. The major expenditure in an RFID implementation is the tags themselves, which can represent about half of the overall cost. As of mid-2004, the price of tags has not moved much from $.80 a piece and it may be some time before the cost comes down to $.50 or less. Tags for DVDs run around $1.50, and tags for VHS tapes approach $2.00. Circulation and staff processing stations are comparable in cost to the components of a typical theft-detection system, around $4,000 each. A server that interfaces between the RFID hardware and the ILS, which is required in most systems, can cost around $15,000. Return drops start at $4,000 and can get quite expensive, depending on the amount of sorting to be done. Since sorters can be customized into any number of configurations, the price range can be very wide. The most expensive piece of library RFID hardware is the self-checkout machine, which starts at $20,000.

It is important to note that not all RFID installations require all the hardware components that have been discussed throughout this chapter. For example, a library may elect not to use return drops or self-checkout machines. The number of each of the hardware devices required for an implementation is dependant on the intended role of the system in the library. For example, a library using the system for inventory purposes but not for circulation would not require a circulation station but may require more hand-held wands. In the end, the cost for an RFID implementation depends entirely on the goals and expectations of the library.

Standards

There are many choices and trade-offs a library must consider when researching the RFID marketplace. The key is buying a system which utilizes tags that meet current standards and can be reprogrammed and used with the majority of RFID readers. This is a library's insurance that the investment the library made in RFID tags will outlast its commitment to the RFID hardware purchased. Unfortunately, different vendors have incorporated different proprietary protocols and standards that do not allow for system interoperability. This lack of standardization in the design and configuration of the tags themselves has led many libraries considering RFID to postpone the investment until a standard emerges.

There is no standard protocol for the data communication between the tag and the various devices, although a number of initiatives are underway. Fortunately, in all current systems the data transfer between the RFID reader and the local ILS adheres to the 3M SIP2 standard. This standard will soon be replaced by the National Information Standards Organization (NISO) NCIP protocol. Efforts are now being made in various standards committees to develop a common RFID protocol that would be a first step toward interoperability of tags and hardware from various vendors.

SELECTING AN RFID SOLUTION

The selection of an RFID system launches a library into a long-term commitment to that system primarily because of its high cost and the time-consuming changes that the library must engage in to successfully use the new system. The decision to utilize RFID technology requires that a library investigate all vendor solutions to determine which one works best for its needs. There are many questions to ask, including the following:

- What is the goal of the library's installation? (circulation, stacks maintenance, etc.)
- Which materials are to be tagged? (books, journals, audiovisual materials)
- How many volumes or items need to be tagged?
- What year was the vendor's RFID product line introduced?
- How many installations are there of the system? Where are they?
- Was the tag specifically designed for library use?
- How many circulation and processing stations will be needed?
- How many public exits will require security gates?
- How many shelf-reading wands are needed?
- Will self-checkout stations be used?
- Will return chutes be used? Is a sorting station desired?
- Is the library a part of any consortium? Will the library require the use of RFID and bar codes to continue involvement in that consortium?

Finally, since the financial and human-resource impact of an RFID implementation can be substantial, the library community needs to begin to conduct a comprehensive assessment of the technology to enable librarians to make the best possible decisions involving the implementation of this technology. The community also needs to begin to actively monitor and shape the direction that vendors are taking with RFID systems designed for libraries to ensure that they are meeting the unique needs of libraries.

PRIVACY

Historically, libraries have been very diligent in protecting customer borrowing records. The presence of an RFID chip has resulted in some debate regarding the potential intrusion on the privacy library customers have traditionally expected. Can RFID be used to track a customer's movements and reading habits? Will information be gathered and used to market unwanted products and services to the library customer, either by the library or perhaps by someone else reading the tag?

RFID is no different in its impact on our privacy than debit-card systems, cell phones, gas passes, toll tags, or credit cards. A number of technical factors work against collecting information about customers and their reading habits and preferences without their consent. The first is read range. All of the major RFID systems currently deployed in libraries use 13.56 MHz technology. At this frequency, the read range a system can achieve and still stay within governmental regulations is fairly short (typically, no more than a few feet). Therefore, tracking customers and collecting information on their interests during a library visit would require an array of RFID readers. Installing large numbers of readers would not be economically feasible for most libraries.

Information about items a customer borrows is collected during the checkout process. However, this is not unique to RFID-enabled libraries. Every library charges borrowed items to customers, typically via an entry in a circulation database. Many libraries erase information about items borrowed once they are returned, in deference to customer privacy and to protect a customer's privacy against investigations supported by the Patriot Act. These processes are no different when RFID is used as the checkout mechanism.

Privacy advocates are concerned that information about who borrowed an item could be stored on the RFID tag affixed to items. While it is technically possible to do so, it is not really practical due to the limited memory capacity of present RFID chips. No library RFID system on the market today records any customer information on the RFID tag itself. They do not provide any information beyond what the library had already recorded in its circulation database. When the capabilities and limitations of RFID technology are carefully examined, the possibilities for abuse are minimal.

NORTH AMERICAN RFID VENDORS

Bibliotheca (URL: http://www.bibliotheca-rfid.com/)

Checkpoint Systems :URL:http://www.checkpointsystems.com/content/library/)

ID Systems (URL: http://www.idsystems-dialoc.com/)

Tagsys (URL: http://www.tagsys.net/)

3M Library Systems (URL: http://www.3m.com/library/)

Libramation (URL: http://www.libramation.com/)

FURTHER READING

Boss, Richard W. (2003, November/December). RFID technology for libraries. *Library Technology Reports, 39*(6), 6–58.

Dorman, David. (2003, December). RFID poses no problem for customer privacy. *American Libraries, 34* (11), 86.

Dorman, David. (2003, October). RFID on the Move. *American Libraries, 34*(9), 72–73.

E-ZPass. Available at: http://www.ezpass.com/.

Fabbi, Jennifer L, Watson, Sidney D., and Marks, Kenneth E. (2002). Implementation of the 3M Digital Identification System at the UNLV libraries. *Library Hi Tech, 20*(1), 104–110.

Flagg, Gordon. (2003, December). Should libraries play tag with RFIDs? *American Libraries, 34*(11), 69–71.

Lindquist, Mats G. (2003). RFID in libraries—Introduction to the issues. *69th IFLA General Conference and Council, Berlin, Germany, 1–9 August 2003*. URL: http://www.ifla.org/IV/ifla69/papers/161e-Lindquist.pdf. (Accessed July 6, 2005.)

McArthur, Alastair. (2003). Integrating RFID into library systems—Myths and realities. *69th IFLA General Conference and Council, Berlin, Germany, 1–9 August 2003*. URL: http://www.ifla.org/Ivifla69/papers/130e-McArthur.pdf. (Accessed July 6, 2005).

Murray, Peter E. (2004). The radio frequency revolution: Tips and trends for implementing RFID systems in libraries. *ALA Annual Conference, Orlando, Florida, June 28, 2004.* URL: http://www.pandc.org/peter/presentations/ala-2004-rfid/PMurray-ala-ac-2004-rfid.pdf. (Accessed July 6, 2005.)

National Information Standards Organization. *ANSI/NISO Z39.83 -2002 Circulation Interchange Part 1: Protocol (NCIP)*. URL: http://www.niso.org/standards/standard_detail.cfm?std_id = 728. (Accessed July 6, 2005.)

Oder, Norman. (2003). "RFID Use Raises Privacy Concerns: Tags Help Foster Circulation and Fight Theft; Standards Needed." *Library Journal 128*, (19), 19–20.

Schuyler, Michael. (2004, January). RFID: Helpmate or Conspiracy? *Computers in Libraries, 24*(1), 22–24.

Smart, Laura J. *RFID in Libraries*. URL: http://www.libraryrfid.net.

Speedpass. URL: http://www.speedpass.com/.

Sullivan, Laurie. (2004, May 18). "Wal-Mart maps RFID expansion plans." *Information Week.* URL: http://www.informationweek.com/story/showArticle.jhtml?articleID = 20600021. (Accessed July 6, 2005.)

Want, Roy. (2004, January). RFID. A key to automating everything. *Scientific American, 290*(1), 56–65.

Ward, Diane M. (2004, March). "Helping you buy: RFID." *Computers in Libraries, 24*(3), 19–20, 22–4.

Yue, Joseph. (2004, Spring). Implementing RFID. *Colorado Libraries, 30*(1), 35–6.

GLOSSARY

Antenna

Antennas are the conductive elements that radiate and/or receive energy in the-radio frequency spectrum, to and from the tag.

Data Rate (Data Transfer Rate)

In a radio frequency identification system, the rate at which data is communicated between the tag and the reader. Usually measured in bits per second (bps).

EEPROM (Electrically Erasable Programmable Read-Only Memory)

A nonvolatile storage device on microchips. RFID tags that use EEPROM are more expensive than factory-programmed tags, but they offer more flexibility because the end user can write an ID number to the tag at the time the tag is going to be used.

Electromagnetic Field

An electromagnetic field is produced when electrically charged particles are set in motion. The frequency of an electromagnetic field is measured in Hertz and is related to its wavelength.

Frequency

RFID tags use low, high, ultra-high frequencies. Each frequency has advantages and disadvantages that make them more suitable for some applications than for others.

High Frequency Tags

RFID tags that communicate with readers operating at 13.56MHz range.

Low Frequency Tags

RFID tags that communicate with readers operating in the 125–134KHz range.

Memory

The amount of data that can be stored on a tag.

Passive Tags

Passive tags contain no internal power source. They are externally powered and typically derive their power from the carrier signal radiated from the scanner.

Power Levels

The amount of radio frequency energy radiated from a reader or an active tag. The higher the power output, the longer the read range.

Programming

Writing data to a tag.

RFID

Systems that read or write data to radio frequency tags through the use of the use of inductive coupling.

Range

The distance at which successful reading and/or writing can be accomplished.

Read-only Tags

Tags that contain data that cannot be changed unless the microchip is reprogrammed electronically.

Read Rate

The maximum rate at which data can be read from a tag, expressed in bits or bytes per second.

Read/Write

Tags that allow new data or revisions to data to be entered into the tag are called read/write tags, memory cards, or memory modules.

Reader (also called an interrogator)

A device that extracts information from the RFID tag.

Scanner

The antenna's transmitter (or exciter) and receiver electronics integrated in a single package called the scanner. They may be combined with additional digital electronics, including a microprocessor, in a package called a reader.

Sensor

Sensors are increasingly being combined with RFID tags to detect the presence of materials at an identifiable location.

Smart Label

A label that contains an RFID tag. It is considered "smart" because it can store information, such as a unique serial number, and communicate with a reader.

Transponder

A radio transmitter-receiver that is activated when it receives a predetermined signal. RFID tags are sometimes referred to as transponders.

Ultra High Frequency (UHF) Tags

RFID tags that communicate with readers operating in the 869–930MHz range

Write Rate

The rate at which information is transferred to a tag, written into the tag's memory, and then verified as being correct. It is quantified as the average number of bits or bytes per second in which the complete transaction can be performed.

6

BLOGS AND RSS

Darlene Fichter and H. Frank Cervone

Often, innovative technologies seem to come out of nowhere. The microwave oven and Post-It Notes are examples of this. At the time they were invented, no one really knew that there was a need for such technology, and no one was asking for such items. However, imagine what our lives would be like today without either!

Other technologies, such as the revolving door, arose under slightly different circumstances. In this case, a problem had been identified (the inability to get people into and out of a building quickly), but existing solutions were not adequate. Someone, however, discarded their preconceived notions of entrée and egress from a building and went about solving the problem.

Weblogs, or *blogs* as they are more commonly known, came about as the result of this last model of innovation. A particular set of forces at a distinct time in the development of the World Wide Web gave rise to a breakthrough in thinking about a problem. That problem was how to provide an easy, quickly learned means of updating Web content that did not require complex software or large numbers of system staff.

A blog is, for the most part, a fairly simple concept. It is a Web page that contains brief, frequently updated entries arranged in chronological order. What makes blogging software special is that it allows anyone, as long as they can click a mouse and type, to produce a Web page containing content that can be updated easily as circumstances require.

Not too surprisingly, these people who create blogs are referred to as bloggers. And the blogs they produce have widely ranging scope, complexity, and depth. Many blogs are personal journals, but other blogs cover news and events while providing commentary and context. Blogs are available on

a wide range of topics, including law, technology, specialized scholarly interests, local school issues, and issues related to libraries. Although blogs can be
trivial and ridiculous, such as those related to the pets of celebrities, they can
also provide useful information not available anywhere else.

Given that blogs are specifically designed to promote content creation in
an easy-to-use manner, it is not surprising that Evan Williams, the creator
of the software program Blogger, has described blogs as being about three
things: frequency, brevity, and personality (Turnbull, 2001). According to
him, these three characteristics are the driving factors in the popularity of
blogs as a publishing format.

An inherent assumption of blogs is that they are updated frequently.
While there are no hard-and-fast rules in this matter, in many cases blogs are
updated daily; many blogs, however, are updated several times a day, or even
hourly. The entries in the blog are also usually brief and point to another Web
site, a news story, or some other item of interest that contains more detailed
information about the topic at hand.

Although most blogs have the capability of functioning as a news feed
(through a Rich Site Summary, or RSS), what differentiates a blog from a
simple news feed is that most blogs have a distinctive voice or perspective.
Many blogs are intentionally not objective. The voice that a blog takes on can
vary considerably. It may be sarcastic, funny, witty, erudite, expert, explor-
atory, bumbling, in a factual news-reporting style, or any combination of
these. Because blogs do tend to show some personality, they can be very
engaging reading.

The use of blogs has expanded dramatically since 2000. A major factor in
this has been the advent of Web sites that offer blogging software for free
as well as the tools and storage space for the blog entries. These blogging
software Web sites made it extremely easy for anyone to publish and maintain a Web page, because they eliminated the need to know how to design
pages in HTML and how to transfer the pages to the server with FTP. With
a Web browser and username/password combination, a person can add content from anywhere, at anytime, as long as they have access to an Internet
connection. Creation of a blog is further eased by the use of a template, supplied by the blogging-software provider, and the look and tone of the blog
can be customized with the inclusion of such things as the name of the blog
and photographs.

Blogs and news feeds via RSS have received heightened media attention
recently. Some of this attention is due to the number of more established technology companies that have moved into the blogging-software business. An
example of this, and one of the most talked about moves in the industry, was
the purchase of the *Blogger* software by Google in 2003 (Gillmor, 2003).

Blogs also played a large role in the Democratic primaries of 2004, attract-
ing both media attention and commentary (Kapp, 2004). Also in 2004, book
publishing ventured into the realm of blogging, printing a number of books
that are aggregations of posts from intriguing blog sites (Radosh, 2004).

Libraries and librarians have also caught blogging fever. From a mere handful of librarian blogs, such as Jenny Levine's *The Shifted Librarian* (http://www.theshiftedlibrarian.com/) to Blake Carver's *LISNews* (http://lisnews.com/), blogging has flourished into several hundred library-related blogs worldwide, such as *Catalogablog* at http://catalogablog.blogspot.com/ by David Bigwood (United States), *Bibliotecarios sem fronteiras* at http://biblio.crube.net/index.php by Viviane Silva in Brazil, and *Fermo2003* at http://fermo2003.blogspot.com/ coordinated by Giovanni Bergamin (Italy).

HOW EASY IS IT TO PUBLISH A BLOG?

Many people, when first hearing about a blog, do not realize how easy it is to create one. To demonstrate how easy it really is, the following example walks through how to set up a blog (using the free, Web-based software *Blogger*) and create the first post. It will become clear why blogs have caught on so quickly. This new blog and its first entry can be created in less than five minutes with no specific technical know-how required.

The process of creating the blog starts by going to the host site, http://www.blogger.com, and then clicking on "Create Your Blog Now." Once the Web page displays, the Web form should be completed by entering the requested information into the four fields: *username, password, display name* (which will show when you post your blog entries), and *e-mail address* (Figure 6.1).

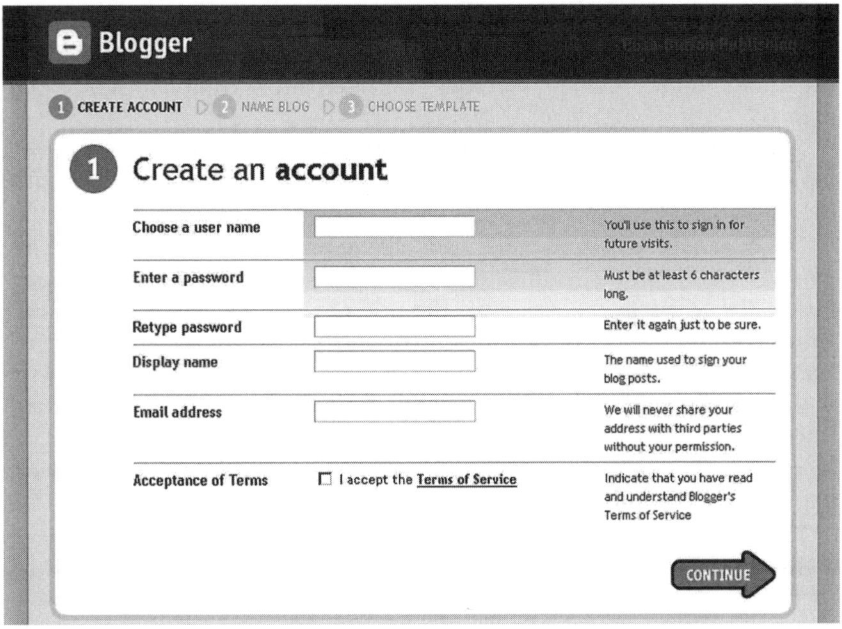

Figure 6.1 Creating a Blog Account

Figure 6.2 Naming Your Blog

Next, the blog must be named. This can be several words but should prob-ably be kept to a short phrase that will be memorable, because this will be the text that uniquely identifies your Weblog address at blogspot.com (Figure 6.2). For example, "Library Weblogs" is named http://libweblogs.blogspot. com.

The next page (Figure 6.3) asks the blogger to choose a template or a design for the blog pages. At this point, the blog has been created and is ready to accept the first entry—the first blog posting.

The blog editing window (Figure 6.4) requires that two information fields, *title* and *post,* be completed. The title field is, not surprisingly, for the head-line of the entry. In this example, the title of the entry will be "Economic Impact of Libraries." The post field is where the body of the entry is typed. Formatting is possible because the Web form has a Microsoft Word–style toolbar that provides functional buttons for styling type as bold and italic, inserting a URL, and creating block quotes. Once the entry is created, it can be published immediately or saved as a draft. Once published, the entry can be viewed immediately (Figure 6.5).

This step-by-step example demonstrates how quickly anyone can set up a basic Weblog and start posting. However, this example just scratched the surface of what is possible. Many bloggers go beyond the basic features, by customizing the template for their site, completing the corporate profile

Figure 6.3 Choosing a Design

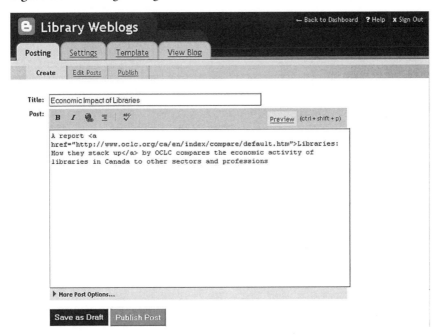

Figure 6.4 The Blog Editing Window

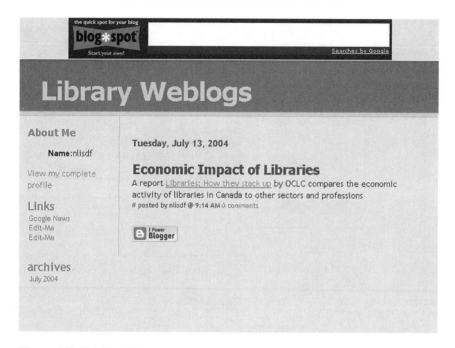

Figure 6.5 The Final Blog

page, adding side menu links, and incorporating other advanced features. More sophisticated bloggers might want to have their blog hosted directly on their own Web site. In that case, the blogger would complete the advanced options to set up FTP or SFTP (secure file transfer protocol), which enables their blog entries to be automatically copied to their Web site.

RSS

RSS is an important component of blog software because it has become the de facto standard for publishing syndication information on the Web. Before RSS, Web site developers who wanted to offer headlines and links to news feeds on their site were faced with the time-consuming task of trying to retrieve, merge, and integrate news services from a variety of producers in a wide range of formats. Each site that produced news headline information was unique, which required the aggregator to write a special parser to interpret the HTML pages and extract relevant content. Particularly onerous was that whenever the format of the parsed Web page changed, the program interpreting that page had to be modified as well.

Given this environment, when Netscape developed RSS to set up its news channels at Netscape Netcenter (http://www.mynetscape.com), other

Web developers took note. Because Netscape shared the format with other news agencies, RSS is used today on sites such as Slashdot, Forbes, CNET, News.com, Wired, CNN, and ZDNet. RSS arrived just in time to meet the pressing need of producers of Web content to share their news in an inexpensive manner and attract more readers to their sites. RSS made it easy to share and aggregate news stories from a variety of suppliers by providing a list of standard elements that are used to describe the news source and the headlines.

As can be seen in the RSS coding from the Northwestern University Library's "In the Spotlight" feed (Figure 6.6), RSS is both human- and machine-readable. Within that file, it can be seen that there are two major placeholders for data: the *channel* and *item* elements.

The channel element must contain the following:

- Title or name of the channel
- Short description of the channel
- Link to the Web site of the channel
- The language encoding the Web site

Numerous optional elements can be included with the channel, such as copyright, Webmaster, publication date, and so on.

An RSS file can have only one channel element, but it can have up to 15 item elements. Item elements are used to store the headlines and are the meat of the document. These contain title, link, and description elements.

As more and more sites have begun to offer RSS feeds, tools called "news readers" (not to be confused with the old usenet newsreaders) have developed that allow people to subscribe to their favorite RSS feeds. With a reader, one can quickly skim headlines for items of interest and then go to the items of specific interest. In this respect, news readers offer a service similar in nature to a table-of-contents awareness service, but for blogs and RSS feeds. These news readers make it quick and easy to keep up with new articles and blog postings on dozens of sites. While there are dozens of RSS news readers available, both as open source (that is, freely available) and from commercial vendors, a recommended reader for those just getting started is *Bloglines* (http://www.bloglines.com).

BLOGS AND THEIR USE IN LIBRARIES

Blogs can be used in many ways. One way to look at blogs is by type—personal or organizational. Personal blogs are usually created by an individual or group interested in a particular subject area, often a professional interest. Often, these blogs are created outside of work hours and are not a mandated activity of the person's (or persons') employer.

```xml
<?xml version="1.0" encoding="iso-8859-1" ?>
- <rss version="2.0" xmlns:dc="http://purl.org/dc/elements/1.1/" xmlns:sy="http://purl.org/rss/1.0/modules/syndication/"
  xmlns:admin="http://webns.net/mvcb/" xmlns:rdf="http://www.w3.org/1999/02/22-rdf-syntax-ns#"
  xmlns:content="http://purl.org/rss/1.0/modules/content/">
  - <channel>
    <title>In the Spotlight</title>
    <link>http://www.library.northwestern.edu/news/</link>
    <description>News from Northwestern University Library</description>
    <dc:language>en-us</dc:language>
    <dc:creator>p-strait@northwestern.edu</dc:creator>
    <dc:date>2004-07-16T13:47:51-06:00</dc:date>
    <admin:generatorAgent rdf:resource="http://www.movabletype.org/?v=2.63" />
    <sy:updatePeriod>hourly</sy:updatePeriod>
    <sy:updateFrequency>1</sy:updateFrequency>
    <sy:updateBase>2000-01-01T12:00+00:00</sy:updateBase>
    - <item>
      <title>Children's book illustrations on exhibit</title>
      <link>http://www.library.northwestern.edu/news/archives/000485.html</link>
      <description>O Gato e O Escuro (The Cat and the Dark) illustrated by Danuta Wojciechowska and written by Mia Couto
      (Editorial Caminho, 2001, 2003)Orange cats jumping over a dark moon. A cool fish waving a top hat. A kindhearted
      monster...</description>
      - <content:encoded>
        - <![CDATA[
          <p><img alt="gato2.jpg" src="http://www.library.northwestern.edu/news/archives/gato2.jpg" width="250"
          height="290" border="0" /><br /></p>
          <b><p class="caption"><i>O Gato e O Escuro </i>(The Cat and the Dark) illustrated by Danuta Wojciechowska and
          <p>The lively work of childrenʼs book illustrators from around the world will be on display at Northwestern U
          <p>The Hans Christian Andersen Awards are presented every two years by the International Board on Books for Y
          <p>Jeffrey Garrett of Northwestern University Library served as president of the 2004 Hans Christian Andersen
```

Figure 6.6 An example of RSS coding

Organizational blogging can occur internally, inside the firewall on an intranet, or externally for the benefit of the organization's constituents. Blogs in these cases are used for various activities, including project tracking, knowledge sharing, promotion of events or to publish news.

On a different level, blogs can be managed either as a closed activity by a single blogger or a group of related people or as a community blog, which is open to anyone interested enough to register and post entries.

Libraries have started to exploit blog software and take advantage of this easy means of publishing and distributing content. Many libraries use blogs to promote library events and services, while others use a blog as an internal mechanism for distributing news, coordinating work processes, and other activities related to organizational knowledge sharing. The ways libraries are using Weblogs are quite varied.

Library News and Marketing

The Waterboro Public Library (Maine) maintains a blog of literary and library-related news and resources called *h20boro lib blog* (http://www.waterborolibrary.org/blog.htm). This blog provides a way for the library to keep its local community informed about significant developments in these areas.

Although used extensively for internal processes, the most visible use of blog software at the Northwestern University Library is for the "In the Spotlight" feature of the Library's public Web site (http://www.library.northwestern.edu/news/). Using software from the blogging application *Movable Type,* the library's director of public relations is able to publish the blog on the their main Web site, thereby taking advantage of blog software's ease of use and fairly seamless integration.

Taking this approach even further, the Moraine Valley Community College Robert E. Turner Library Learning Resources Center (http://www.morainevalley.edu/lrc/blogs.htm) offers four library blogs for their community, each focused on a different aspect of information: Library News (for the general public), Resources and Search Tips (for students), Construction Updates (for the college community), and the Frankenstein Exhibit (for the general public).

Sharing Knowledge

Some libraries have set up internal or intranet blogs to facilitate knowledge sharing. At the University of Saskatchewan Libraries, Data Library Services has an internal Weblog for sharing reference questions and answers, tips, instructions for downloading files, and other common issues related to providing service. This has helped new staff locate information when another more senior colleague is not available. It has also helped reduce e-mail overload and folders that track tidbits of information.

At the Northwestern University Library, the use of blogs has been spread throughout the Library intranet as a means for coordinating complex work processes. Several groups and committees, including the Web Advisory Group, the Digital Library Committee, the SFX/MetaLib Implementation Group, and others, use blogs as a vehicle for communication and work coordination.

A slightly different use of blog software for knowledge sharing is demonstrated by Randy Reichardt and Geoff Harder, science librarians at the University of Alberta Science and Technology Library, who maintain a blog, *The SciTech Library Question* (http://stlq.info/)that provides information and commentary "of interest to engineering and scitech librarians."

Interactive and Community Services

The Roselle (Illinois) Public Library uses blog software for their *Blogger Book Club* (http://www.roselle.lib.il.us/YouthServices/BookClub/BookClub.htm), an interactive, online book-discussion group for children in grades 4–6. The use of blog software has enabled the library to create an environment where children can share information and have fun in a closed, safe virtual space.

The University of Minnesota Libraries blog project, *U-Think* (http://blog.lib.umn.edu/), has taken blog-software support into an entirely new direction in the academic environment. Intended to support teaching and learning as well as new models of scholarly communication, the library has assumed leadership on campus for blog services, making it possible for anyone on the campus to create their own blog in library-supported and library-maintained space.

Other Uses

Several blog directories provide additional examples of how libraries are using blogs in new and innovative ways:

- *Libdex.* Library blogs listed geographically by country (http://www.libdex.com/weblogs.html)
- *Open Directory Library and Information Science Weblogs.* Alphabetical list of personal, organizational and collaborative library blogs (http://dmoz.org/Reference/Libraries/Library_and_Information_Science/Weblogs/)
- *Blog Without a Library.* Organized by type of library (http://www.blogwithoutalibrary.net/index.shtml?links.html)

BLOG FEATURES

As seen in the prior examples, blog software offers an array of features, functions, and applications for bloggers and blog readers. Some blog programs offer only basic features, while other software offers advanced and obscure functionality that is of use only for very complex sites.

Some features of blog software, such as automatically moving new entries off the home page of the blog and into an archive, are built in. But blog software does differ dramatically in functionality. This is why it is important for the blogger to define what features are important—to provide a guide for blog software selection.

In Figure 6.7, which is the home page of Sabrina I. Pacifici's *beSpacific* Weblog (http://www.bespacific.com/), some of the most important features for most bloggers are demonstrated. These features include:

1. *Date.* The date and, optionally, time of the posting
2. *Headline.* The title of the posting.
3. *Permanent link.* This feature provides a URL to the blog entry that will work, even when the post moves off the main page and into the archives. With this feature, others can link and comment on the posting and use the permanent link as the pointer to the blog entry.
4. *Topics.* Some blogging toolkits can create an index of the archives by topics as well as by date.

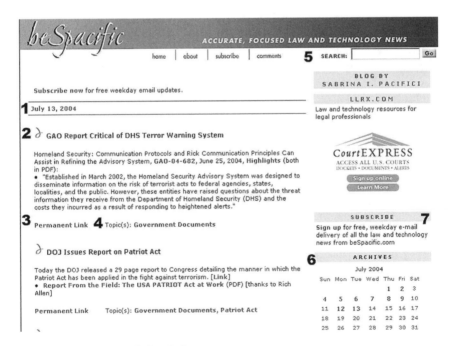

Figure 6.7 Features of Blog Software

5. *Search.* Provides a built-in function to search blog entries by keyword

6. *Archives.* Depending on the software, daily, weekly, monthly, yearly, or topical archives can be created from old postings

Other, more advanced, features can also be useful in various blogs:

- *E-mail subscription.* Allows a blog reader to receive posts by e-mail, either as individual posts or as a daily digest of all posts.

- *Blogroll.* A list of other blogs the blogger finds interesting and visits on a regular basis.

- *RSS feeds.* Provides for the automatic production of an RSS feed of the blog headlines and links.

- *Comments.* Allows visitors to leave a comment about a post and browse the comments left by others.

- *Trackback.* Makes it possible to know who is referencing the various blog postings. This provides a mechanism that lets both the blogger and the blog reader know what other people are saying about a posting. A trackback occurs if another blogger comments on an entry in the blog and has trackback functionality within their blog software enabled. In this case, a notification can be sent to the originating blog, which registers it in a trackback list of links.

- *Long entries.* This feature makes it possible to have a short descriptive entry as well as a longer entry, which could be an entire article or essay,

- *Draft mode.* As the title implies, enables the author to save a post in draft mode, allowing it to be modified and posted later.

- *Spell check.* A handy feature for the lexically challenged.

- *Timed release.* Allows entries to be prepared in advance for posting at a later time.

- *Bookmarklet* or *Browser toolbar.* These tools allow the blogger to automatically capture the URL and title of a Web page and place them into the blog editing form by simply clicking a button (or bookmark). The blogger can then create additional descriptive information.

- *Multiple authors.* This feature is especially important for blogs created or maintained by more than one person, because it allows blogs to be edited and managed by a group of people and gives the ability to track who has done what.

- *Post by e-mail or instant messenger.* For bloggers on the go, new entries can be added by either sending an e-mail to a special blog address or through an instant-messaging client software program.

CHOOSING BLOG SOFTWARE

Although commercial software is available, the majority of bloggers use one of the many free or inexpensive blog software packages. The major decision most bloggers find themselves confronting is whether they should install the blog software locally or instead use a hosted blogging service like Blogger. Certainly, for trying out blogging software, a hosted blog service works well, because it is fast, easy, and usually free (or has a free trial period).

In the long run however, the blogger must weigh the convenience of using a hosted service against the extra work of having internal staff install and maintain blog software. For production services, a hosted blogging service (particularly a free service) may not be suitable, since free hosted blogging services can become overloaded, go offline unexpectedly, or, in the worst case, simply cease to exist.

A compromise between these two options is offered by some hosted services, usually in the form of an advanced feature. The blog entries are created on the hosted service, but the entries are transferred via FTP to a local service. This allows the blogger to use the software of a hosted service, such as Blogger, for editing and maintaining entries but keep the blog pages on a local server within the library's domain name.

In many cases the nature of the blog will dictate whether a hosted service is appropriate or not. Typically, intranet blogs, which contain confidential and sensitive information, must reside inside the firewall.

Currently, these are some of the most popular hosted blogging services:

- Blogger   http:// www.blogger.com
- LiveJournal   http://www.livejournal.com
- TypePad   http://www.typepad.com (fee based)

Many locally installed blog applications are based on open source software: the PHP programming language and the MySQL database system. In most cases they can be installed on Windows-, Linux-, or Unix-based Web servers.

An important factor when selecting a locally installed blog application is whether the site will run a single blog or multiple blogs. While some packages automatically allow for the creation of multiple blogs, a good number of the blog application packages require a separate instance (i.e., running copy of the program) for each Weblog. This model is less desirable because it requires a significant amount of additional on-going software maintenance; it does, however, allow a library to keep the blogs completely independent.

Some of the more popular locally installed blog applications are listed in Table 6.1.

In addition to the models described so far, there are a handful of packages that can be installed on a desktop computer. Once editing of the entries has been completed, the software uses FTP to upload the Weblog files to a Web server. A selection of these types of software packages are listed in Table 6.2.

Once a platform has been chosen and the number of blogs that will be run is determined, there are still several questions that need to be asked in

Table 6.1
Locally installed server-based blog applications

Blogging application	URL	Requirements: language, database
Movable Type	http://www.movabletype.org	Perl, MySQL, or PostgreSQL, or SQLite, or Berkeley DB
PHP-Nuke	http://phpnuke.org/	PHP4.1, MySQL
B2	http://cafelog.com/	PHP4, MySQL database
ExpressionEngine	http://www.pmachine.com/ expressionengine	PHP 4.1, MySQL
Nucleus	http://nucleuscms.org/	PHP4, MySQL
WordPress	http://wordpress.org	PHP4.1, MySQL

Table 6.2
Desktop-computer blog applications

Blogging application	URL	Platform
CityDesk	http://www.fogcreek.com/CityDesk/	Windows
Flog	http://homepage.mac.com/ fromconcentrate/Flog	Macintosh
iBlog	http://www.lifli.com/Products/iBlog/ main.htm	Any operating system with Java
Tinderbox	http:// www.eastgate.com/Tinderbox/	Macintosh

order to narrow the choice of software down to a handful of options. If the blog software will be installed locally, the *Blog Software Chart* (http://www.asymptomatic.net/blogbreakdown.htm) will be a useful tool, because it compares features and services of 15 popular packages. If the blog will be hosted, the *Weblog Compendium* (http://www.lights.com/weblogs/) provides a list of blog-hosting services and blog tools.

SUMMARY

Blogs are Web pages that contain brief, frequently updated entries arranged in chronological order. Many blogs take the form of personal journals, whereas other blogs cover news and events while providing commentary and context. Most blogs have functionality that allows them to publish the headlines as an

RSS news feed. RSS is an important component of blog software because it has become the de facto standard for publishing syndicated information on the Web.

Libraries have started to exploit blog software and take advantage of this easy means of publishing and distributing content. Many libraries use blogs to promote library events and services, while others use a blog as an internal mechanism for distributing news, coordinating work processes, and facilitating other organizational knowledge-sharing activities.

Blog software offers an array of features and functions for bloggers and blog readers. Some blog software features, such as automatically moving new entries off the home page of the blog and into an archive, are built in. However, blog software applications do differ dramatically in functionality. While commercial blogging software is available, the majority of bloggers use one of the many free or inexpensive blog software packages.

Given the large number of free and inexpensive services available, it is easy to get started with blogging, so there is no excuse for not creating your first blog today!

REFERENCES

Gillmor, Dan. (2003, February 15). Google buys Pyra: Blogging goes big-time. *eJournal.* URL: http://weblog.siliconvalley.com/column/dangillmor/archives/000802.shtml#000802.

Kapp, Bonney. (2004, May 19). Campaign blogs outlive candidates. *CBSNews.com Campaign.* URL: http://www.cbsnews.com/stories/2004/05/19/politics/main618477.shtml.

Radosh, Daniel. (2004, May 31). A book in you. *The New Yorker.* URL: http://www.newyorker.com/printable/?talk/040531ta_talk_radosh.

Turnbull, Giles. (2001, February 28). The state of the blog. *Writetheweb.* URL: http://writetheweb.com/Members/gilest/old/107/view.

7

INTRODUCTION TO XML

Art Rhyno

After the invention of the printing press, writers soon found themselves making handwritten notes on freshly printed manuscripts. The notes were needed to instruct printers on typesetting and other production issues. Modern punctuation, which grew out of this practice, can be thought of as an early form of *markup,* literally a technique for identifying structural and contextual aspects of a document.

By the time that documents came to be produced digitally, it was necessary to embed control codes or macros to cause the document to appear as the content creators desired. Early text-processing documents often prominently displayed these codes in the text itself, for example:

.SK 1

Early text-processing and emerging word-processing systems require codes to control formatting, and these codes are called markup:

.TB 4
.OF 4
.SK 1

Generic coding, which began in the late 1960s, was an attempt to use descriptive tags, such as "heading," instead of nonintuitive codes that were often specific to a particular system or printer, such as the ".SK" in the example. William Tunnicliffe and Norman Scharpf of the Graphic Communications Association (GCA) Composition Committee, and a New York book designer named Stanley Rice, who had proposed the idea of a universal catalog of parameterized editorial tags, were key players in establishing a generic coding project in the GCA Composition Committee.[1]

With some help from the corporation IBM, the GCA developed the Generalized Markup Language (GML) in 1969, based on the generic coding ideas of Rice and Tunnicliffe. In addition to being a simple tagging scheme, where tags were identified with "<" and ">" characters, such as <heading>, GML introduced the notion of a formally defined document *type* that would be described with a set of rules. This concept became known as validation, which meant that documents could now be checked to see if they were constructed properly. The use of tags also helped move the presentation decisions associated with documents, such as whether a heading should be bolded, outside of the content-creation process. IBM proved its commitment to using markup by adopting GML for its own large collection of technical documents.

In 1978 the American National Standards Institute (ANSI) committee on Information Processing established the Computer Languages for the Processing of Text committee, a project for a text-description language standard based on GML. The first working draft of the Standard Generalized Markup Language (SGML)[2] was published in 1980 and quickly became adopted on a large scale to help manage and standardize the often vast amounts of documents that are published internally in large organizations.

Tim Berners-Lee, the inventor of the World Wide Web, turned to SGML in the late 1980s to form the basis of a new markup language to support linking content across networks.[3] The result was HyperText Markup Language (HTML),[4] a simple application of SGML with the capability to tie together disparate documents. HTML coincided with the growing popularity of a global network that came to be called the Internet. Together, HTML and the Internet would spark the creation of the biggest publishing system, and also the largest use of markup, ever to be seen since the invention of the printing press and the first scribblings of manuscript authors.

THE PROBLEM WITH HTML

HTML is amazingly successful for creating widely accessible documents, but unlike many other SGML applications, HTML addresses both the presentation of content and its structure. In other words, many HTML tags are selected on the basis of how they cause Web content to appear on a browser. This becomes a problem in the same way that markup commands like ".SK 1" caused difficulties with early electronic documents. For example, if a Web page contains HTML markup like <H1>Introduction to XML</H1> a human reader could presumably tell that the content is an introduction. However, if there were hundreds of documents that contained significant subject information, the difficulty starts to arise if some authors choose to use tags like <H3> XML and Libraries—a totally different introduction</H3>.

If you want to use a program to extract subject information, or even if you just want consistency in subject assignment, it becomes difficult without a commonly used tag like <subject> to mark, or delimit, where this information is contained. As an application of SGML, HTML is limited to a fixed set of tags. In this case, <subject> is not considered a valid HTML tag and cannot be added without convincing browser maintainers that it is a good idea.

Just as important is the separation of content and presentation, which is as fundamental to managing large collections of documents today as it was in the 1960s. HTML freely mixes both, which was fine for the early days of the Web, but as Web sites grew from containing several HTML documents to becoming the virtual public face of most organizations, there was a sense that a "Webified" version of SGML was needed.

In 1996 several high-profile figures in the electronic-text world began work on a "simpler and gentler" SGML, which would be called Extensible Markup Language (XML).[5] In 1998, the World Wide Web Consortium (W3C), the body that oversees Web standards, published the XML 1.0 recommendations. XML was greeted with open enthusiasm, in part because harried Web administrators and publishers immediately recognized how useful XML would be. There are essential aspects of XML that are important for libraries:

- *XML is well formed.* Library Web sites and many other repositories of content are very sensitive to scalability issues. Having a few misplaced tags may not be a big headache with a few HTML documents, but this becomes much more problematic when trying to control quality for thousands, or even tens of thousands, of documents. XML helps eradicate sloppy markup, and software is readily available to ensure that an XML document meets baseline requirements.

- *XML can be validated and can ensure consistency.* XML adopts the validation mechanism of SGML called the document type definition (DTD),[6] and also provides additional validation options. Identifying or authoring the appropriate DTD is one of the most important steps in managing a library's digital collection. This establishes a consistency in the content that will help both in the sharing of the content with others and in future migrations.

- *XML separates content from presentation.* Even in the early discussions of the GCA Composition Committee, it was recognized that putting stylistic information in content worked against handing off the presentation layer of content to those with strong design capabilities. Much of the world's content is also produced and maintained without any presentation considerations, and, generally speaking, it usually improves information flow and allows for greater flexibility if presentation details can be applied completely outside of the content-creation process. This is particularly true for organizations like libraries that often manage information from many sources.

We will look at each of these areas in detail.

XML IS WELL FORMED

XML documents consist of elements, tags, and character data. An element is, in fact, made up of tags. There are typically two tags, a start tag,

```
<mytag>
```

and an end tag,

```
</mytag>
```

Notice how the end tag is exactly the same except for the "/" character. XML is unforgiving when it comes to consistency; <mytag> is not the same as <Mytag>, the characters have to match exactly. XML also supports of the concept of empty tags, such as <br/> as a shorthand way to write
</br>. Both forms are considered equivalent.

Elements may be nested, so, for example, there may be a set of tags identifying an author:

```
<mytag>
    <author>Art</author>
    <library>Leddy</library>
</mytag>
```

An XML document must always provide at least one element, and the first one is known as the root element. Elements must also be properly nested in XML, that is, tags must always follow the sequence in which they are introduced. For example:

```
<old_lady>
    <bird>
        <fly/>
    </bird>
</old_lady>
```

All XML elements can have attributes that qualify or enhance the content of the element in some way. These are always attached to the start tag and must be enclosed in either single or double quotation marks. For example, the following element has a created attribute of "2004–07–12":

```
<mytag created = "2004–07–12">
    <author>Art</author>
    <library>Leddy</library>
</mytag>
```

Comments in XML documents use the same syntax as in HTML, beginning with <!— and ending with —>; for example:

```
<!—This is a comment—>
    <mytag created = "2003–07–12">
```

```
<author>Art</author>
<library>Leddy</library>
</mytag>
```

XML uses the concept of entity references, which comes from SGML. There are characters so critical in constructing XML documents that special provision needs to be made to let them be used, or escaped, in the content of elements. For example, the less-than character (<) is used to designate the beginning of a tag and can only appear in the text of an XML document if it is written in this form:

```
&lt;
```

For example:

```
<number_info>
    4 &lt; 5
</number_info>
```

Entity references will be immediately familiar to many users of the Web, where they are common for tasks like specifying spaces (&nbscp;) and other areas where a Web author wants a specific character to appear in a browser. In addition to supporting and allowing the definition of entity references, XML can make use of the concept of a *CDATA* section, a convenience function that allows XML content creators to deal easily with segments of text that might have a lot of characters which would otherwise need to be escaped. These sections are identified by an opening <![CDATA[and end with]]>. This is an example of a CDATA section:

```
<number_info>
    <![CDATA[
      5 > 4
    ]]>
</number_info>
```

Finally, XML uses a special format to identify *processing instructions*. A processing instruction begins with <? and ends with ?>. The word following the opening tag is the target, and it identifies the processing instruction. Everything else is to provide additional information about the instruction. The most well known processing instruction is the XML declaration itself:

```
<?xml version = "1.0" encoding = "UTF-8"?>
```

To summarize, in order to qualify as well formed, an XML document must possess the following characteristics:

1) Ensure that every start tag has a matching end tag
2) Ensure that elements are nested in the proper order

3) Provide at least one root element

4) Ensure that attribute values are quoted

5) Use unique attribute names within the start tag

6) Certain characters, such as <, must be escaped if they occur in an element or attribute, unless they are contained in a CDATA section

7) Comments and processing instructions are to be placed outside of tags

UNDERSTANDING VALIDATION

The difference between a well formed and a valid XML document is that the latter is based on a set of rules for identifying the tags, attributes to be used in a document, as well as what order and combinations are allowed. These rules are often described in a DTD and may be included directly in an XML file; for example:

```
<?xml version = "1.0"?>
<!DOCTYPE author[
<!ELEMENT author      (name,title,email phone)>
<!ELEMENT name        (#PCDATA)>
<!ELEMENT title       (#PCDATA)>
<!ELEMENT email       (#PCDATA)>
<!ELEMENT phone       (#PCDATA)>
]>
<author>
   <name> Melville Louis Kossuth Dewey</name>
   <title>Director, New York State Library</title>
   <email>dewey@nylibrary.org</email>
   <phone>(000) 000–0000</phone>
</author>
```

In this example, the DTD is identified by the DOCTYPE tag, and the DTD rules are described directly. However, it is more common, and usually more convenient, to refer to an external DTD:

```
<?xml version = "1.0"?>
<!DOCTYPE author SYSTEM "author.dtd">
<author>
   <name>Melville Louis Kossuth Dewey</name>
   <title>
Director, New York State Library
   </title>
   <email>
dewey@nylibrary.org </email>
   <phone>(000) 000–0000</phone>
</author>
```

DTDs use the following format to define elements:

<!ELEMENT element_name specification>

The specification for the elements in the examples is PCDATA, which indicates that the elements must contain character (textual) data. DTDs can have little resemblance to the content that they prescribe, and their somewhat cryptic syntax was a major factor in the development of XML Schema,[7] a newer and truly XML-based approach for expressing rules for documents. Most important, XML Schema uses namespaces,[8] a mechanism to distinguish between elements and attributes from different sources (called vocabularies), an important consideration for cases where additional or alternative validation is required.

Take the following XML document as a simple example: :

```
<?xml version = "1.0"?>
<author>Melville Dewey</author>
```

We may still want the author element to contain character data, a requirement we enforced in the DTD using the PCDATA specification. In XML Schema, this requirement can be set as follows:

```
<?xml version = "1.0"?>
<xs:schema xmlns:xsd = "http://www.w3.org/2001/XMLSchema">
    <xs:element name = "author" type = "xs:string"/>
</xs:schema>
```

Note that we use the string type, which is equivalent to PCDATA in a DTD. XML Schema also gives us options for more specific types of data, such as decimal and dateTime. In the example above, the namespace support in XML Schema can be seen by the use of the xmlns attribute, which identifies a URL (http://www.w3.org/2001/XMLSchema) that is associated with the vocabulary. A code is also used, in this case xs, as a way to associate elements throughout the document with the namespace.

XML Schema is capable of more complex validation than DTDs. For example, we could limit the number of characters that could be used to specify an author.

```
<xs:simpleType name = "author">
    <xs:restriction base = "xs:string">
        <xs:maxLength value = "50"/>
    </xs:restriction>
</xs:simpleType>
```

XML Schema can be used for very sophisticated restrictions on the format of content in elements. For example, we could so some checking of ISBNs with a regular expression (a syntax widely used in the computer world as a shorthand for patterns in content):[9]

```
<xs:element name = "isbn">
  <xs:restriction base = "xs:string">
    <xs:pattern value = "\d[-]\d{3,3}[-]\d{5,5}[-][\dX]"/>
  </xs:restriction>
</xs:element>
```

It is important to note that XML Schema is still not as widely supported in XML software as are DTDs. As well, the verboseness and myriad options in XML Schema have not been without its critics, and a full-blown and widely supported alternative to XML Schema is RELAX NG,[10] a mature mechanism for XML validation developed in OASIS (The Organization for the Advancement of Structured Information Standards). Easier to use than XML Schema, with stronger validation capabilities for attributes, RELAX NG is a heavyweight contender for XML validation and has gained a lot of traction for large XML projects.

The good news for libraries is that there are numerous XML vocabularies that have been described with DTDs, XML Schemas, and/or RELAX NG. This provides an immediate starting point to structuring content in a standard manner. It is important to have a sense of how validation works, but in many cases you will be able to plug the appropriate validation specification into an authoring tool or some other software and it will help guide you through the process of creating content in the prescribed format.

The following vocabularies are especially pertinent for libraries. By using validation tools, such as XML editors that understand DTDs, these vocabularies can form a basis for building standardized content.

Vocabulary	Description	Available As
DocBook[11]	DocBook is a popular XML format for prose documents and is often used for technical documentation. A library might use DocBook for maintaining systems documentation and other technical materials.	DTD
Encoded Archival Description (EAD)[12]	EAD is a standard for archival finding aids and is widely used by the Library of Congress and others for this purpose. The standard was developed at the University of California–Berkeley and is now sponsored by the Society of American Archivists.	DTD
Metadata Object Description Schema (MODS)[13]	MODS is a lightweight version of MARC (Machine Readable Cataloguing) that uses language-based cataloguing tags instead of the numeric designations familiar to cataloguers. MODS also regroups some of the elements of MARC 21 and has attracted lot of interest from a broad range of communities interested in bibliographic description.	XML Schema

Open Archives Initiative (OAI)[14]	OAI refers to both a metadata harvesting protocol (more specifically known as OAI-PMH or the *OAI Protocol for Metadata Harvesting*), and is a reference to a group of technologies responsible for managing metadata and associated services. Libraries could use OAI to make metadata available to other sites as well as to take advantage of OAI software to harvest external metadata and build databases. Some Integrated Library System (ILS) providers, such as SIRSI, are also adding OAI capabilities to the library catalogue.	XML Schema
Resource Description Framework (RDF)[15]	RDF is a language and a data modeling architecture for describing metadata, and it is the flagship technology in the W3C's Semantic Web initiative. RDF may be the single most contentious technology topic in the Web community but is worthy of attention from libraries if only because libraries are the world's largest suppliers of metadata and have an enormous stake in whatever approaches are adopted to handle metadata on the Web.	DTD, Relax NG, XML Schema
Really Simple Syndication or RDF Site Summary (RSS)[16]	RSS is the preferred technology for providing information updates, or syndicating news, on the Web. RSS-aware programs called news aggregators have become wildly popular, particularly in the Weblogging/blogging community, where Weblogs often offer an RSS-based option to subscribe to updates. RSS has been used for such library activities as notifying patrons when new books arrive on a particular topic and for providing periodic searches on topics of interest.	DTD, Relax NG, XML Schema
Text Encoding Initiative (TEI)[17]	TEI is a mature and internationally supported XML specification for full text. Libraries involved in any sort of project involving the preparation and management of full-text resources should investigate TEI closely, since a large body of documentation and associated software has been built around it.	DTD
XML Organic Bibliographic Information Schema (XOBIS)[18]	Possibly the most interesting and most ambitious XML-based initiative to bring cataloguing into the frontlines of the Web, XOBIS is an experimental project from Stanford's Lane Library to restructure bibliographic and authority data in XML. XOBIS goes the farthest from a literal mapping of MARC into XML and tries to fully leverage the networked environment that is currently being fueled by the Web and XML.	Relax NG

SEPARATING CONTENT FROM PRESENTATION

XML supports the styling and repurposing of content through a technology called stylesheets, which consist of a broad suite of standards and implementations. Like XML itself, stylesheets have roots in SGML and entered the Web in 1996 when the W3C introduced a standard called Cascading Stylesheets (CSS).[19] Cascading refers to the possible cascade of stylesheets from different sources, and CSS has mechanisms for prioritizing different stylesheet sources. CSS offers Web developers precise control over layout, fonts, colors, backgrounds, and other typographical effects; as well as a way to update the appearance and formatting of an unlimited number of pages by changing just one document. For example, consider a very simple HTML file:

```
<HTML>
<HEAD>
<!—Start Stylesheet Rules—>
<STYLE TYPE = "text/css">
<!—
    H1 { color: green; font-size: 35px; font-family: impact }
—>
</STYLE>
<!—End of Stylesheet Rules—>
<TITLE>Planning for XML at the Library</TITLE>
</HEAD>
<BODY>
<H1>Pay attention</H1>
<P>We will soon be using XML for all activities at the library.</P>
</BODY>
</HTML>
```

CSS uses a series of directives, or rules, to specify how content should be displayed. The rule tells the Web browser that all text surrounded by <H1></H1> should be displayed in green. Each rule consists of a selector and a declaration. In the example above, H1 is the selector and represents the tag that the style will be attached to. The declaration is what defines what the style actually is. The declaration also consists of two parts, the property (in this case, color) and the value (green).

On its own, an embedded style sheet is somewhat useful. But the real advantages come when style sheets are referenced separately. This is done using the <LINK> tag. So if we put our H1 rule in a file called style.css, then we could achieve the same effect by referencing it as shown:

```
<HTML>
<HEAD>
<LINK REL = "stylesheet" HREF = "style.css" TYPE = "text/css">
<TITLE>Planning for XML at the Library</TITLE>
```

```
</HEAD>
<BODY>
<H1>Pay attention</H1>
<P>We will soon be using XML for all activities at the library.</P>
</BODY>
</HTML>
```

You can link to the same stylesheets file from an unlimited number of HTML or XML documents. The XML syntax is similar to what is used in HTML:

```
<?xml-stylesheet type = "text/css" href = "style.css"?>
```

CSS also allows the definition of additions for special processing using a construct called classes. For example, if you wanted some paragraphs in your documents to be red and others to be blue, you can create two classes of P, each with its own rules. The rules (either embedded in the document or in an external file) would look like this:

```
P.red { color: red }
P.blue { color: purple }
```

There are many times when libraries want to do more than ornament the content of documents, and this is where XML-specific stylesheets called XSLT,[20] becomes useful. Using XSLT, you can transform an XML document into any text-based format. For example, consider a very simple XML file:

```
<?xml version = "1.0"?>
<?xml-stylesheet href = "first.xsl" type = "text/xsl"?>
<content>XSLT is the future of Library Web applications</content>
```

To convert it to an HTML document, you could create an XSLT file that looks like this:

```
<?xml version = "1.0"?>
<xsl:stylesheet version = "1.0" xmlns:xsl = "http://www.w3.org/1999/XSL/
Transform">
<xsl:template match = "/">
<html>
<head>
<title>XSLT Example</title>
</head>
<body>
<p><xsl:value-of select = "content"/></p>
</body>
</html>
</xsl:template>
</xsl:stylesheet>
```

Notice the use of the namespace (http://www.w3.org/1999/XSL/Trans-form). Like XML Schema, XSLT supports namespaces, and this is important for XSLT applications to identify how content should be processed. XSLT makes extensive use of a standard called XPath,[21] a separate W3C standard that defines a syntax for locating and extracting any part of an XML document. The select = "content" in the XSLT document above relies on XPath for matching and can be a much more elaborate expression. For example, select = "*/@[starts-with(.,'XSLT')]" will look for any element with an attribute that begins with the characters XSLT.

XSLT documents can be specified directly in an XML file in the same manner as CSS, for example:

<?xml-stylesheet type = "text/xsl" href = "style.xsl"?>

However, client-side styling with XSLT is generally frowned upon at this point, and it is better to use server-side transformations, where the processing takes place on the Web server rather than the patron's browser.

XSLT is a powerful language for transforming content but is often a source of great confusion because the W3C Working Group responsible for creating an Extensible Stylesheet Language (XSL) issued two recommendations, one for transforming information (XSLT), and the XSL Recommendation, also called Formatting/Flow Objects (XSL-FO)[22] for paginating content. However, both are usually expressed together, and most often, a reference to XSL can be thought of as equivalent to XSLT.

As a general rule of thumb for working with stylesheets, if your XML content does not have to be rearranged, use CSS. Otherwise, use XSLT, in one of two ways: either generate the style properties together with the rearranged text, using XSL-FO for producing page-orientated content, or generate a new XML or HTML document, and then provide a CSS style sheet for the new document.

XML TOOLS AND SOFTWARE

XML is the conduit to an amazing quantity and diversity of tools and software. From a practical perspective, XML allows you to leverage a worldwide community's efforts in defining tools and applications for managing content. Even if you came to the conclusion that XML is the most despicable technology in the world, the most gifted and well-funded library technology team would be hard pressed to build even a fraction of the infrastructure that XML immediately taps into. The following list is a starting point to start exploring XML-based software that may be useful for your library.

Application	Description
AxKit[23]/Cocoon[24]	AxKit and Cocoon are two projects of the Apache Foundation, which, among other things, produces the worlds most popular Web server. Both AxKit and Cocoon offer server-side XSLT processing options but are of special interest for their support of "XML-directed" solutions, a methodology that uses stylesheets to reformat data for applications to talk to each other in addition to formatting content for viewing on the Web.
JEdit[25]	There are many freely available, open source (OSS) XML editors, but JEdit is arguably the most mature and has the added benefit of running on every major computing platform. JEdit is a good starting point for staff in libraries to experiment with marking up content.
OpenOffice[26]	OpenOffice offers a well-documented, XML file format for every type of document produced in an office suite, including word-processing files, spreadsheets, and presentations. As organizations that are committed to preserving and extending information, libraries have good reason to promote storage formats that lend themselves to long-term storage and can be repurposed easily. Microsoft Office, and almost every other software application on the planet that is used for content creation, has an XML strategy and some level of XML support, but OpenOffice has a strong lead in this critically important space.
XML Spy[27]	XML Spy is possibly the most widely recognized tool for working with XML and is worth serious consideration for a large XML project. A commercial system with good support for most validation options, including DTDs and XML Schema, XML Spy is a good option for a library that prefers shrink-wrapped software for working with XML.

NOTES

1. See "A Brief History of the Development of SGML" URL: http://www.sgml-source.com/history/sgmlhist.htm.

2. SGML is still a major force in the text processing world A good overview of current activities can be found at the *Cover Pages* Web site. URL: http://xml.cover pages.org/sgml.html.

3. Tim Berners-Lee, *Weaving the Web: The Original Design and Ultimate Destiny of the World Wide Web by its Inventor* (San Francisco: HarperSanFrancisco, 2000).

4. A good starting point for HTML is the *W3C HTML Home Page*. URL: http://www.w3.org/MarkUp/.

5. There are possibly more Web sites dedicated to XML than to any other technology on the Web. A useful and brief synopsis on XML and associated resources is maintained by the W3C. URL: http://www.w3.org/XML/.

6. A concise treatment of DTDs can be found at the amazing *Wikipedia* site. URL: http://en.wikipedia.org/wiki/Document_Type_Definition.

7. XML Schema is also a good showcase for *Wikipedia*. URL: http://en.wikipedia. org/wiki/XML_Schema.

8. The syntax and motivation for namespaces is nicely explained at the *Namespaces in XML* page. URL: http://www.w3.org/TR/REC-xml-names/.

9. A very nice tutorial on regular expressions has been put together by David Mertz at URL: http://gnosis.cx/publish/programming/regular_expressions.html.

10. The main Web site for Relax NG can be found at URL: http://www.relaxng. org.

11. The DocBook home page can be found at URL: http://www.docbook.org.

12. Information on EAD can be found at URL: http://www.loc.gov/ead.

13. The Library of Congress is the maintainer of the MODS standard, see URL: http://www.loc.gov/standards/mods/.

14. The main starting point for OAI is at URL: http://www.openarchives.org.

15. The W3C site for RDF is at URL: http://www.w3.org/RDF. See also *RDF Primer* URL: http://www.w3.org/TR/rdf-primer.

16. Once again, *Wikipedia* is a good starting point for a technology that is widely covered on the web. See URL: http://en.wikipedia.org/wiki/RSS_(protocol).

17. The specification and related documents for TEI can be found at URL: http://www.tei-c.org/.

18. The *Home Page* for XOBIS can be found at URL: http://xobis.stanford.edu. XOBIS is also described in detail in Dick Miller and Kevin S. Clarke, *Putting XML to Work in the Library* (Chicago, IL : American Library Association, 2004).

19. The W3C site for CSS is at URL: http://www.w3.org/Style/CSS/.

20. The specification for XSLT can be found at URL: http://www.w3.org/TR/xslt.

21. XPath is described at URL: http://www.w3.org/TR/xpath.

22. It is probably easier to jump into XSL-FO in practice than to start with the W3C pages. See, for example, *How to Develop Stylesheets for XML to XSL-FO Transformation* URL: http://www.antennahouse.com/XSLsample/XSLsample.htm.

23. AxKit is available from the Apache Foundation. URL: http://axkit.org.

24. Cocoon is available from the Apache Foundation. URL: http://cocoon. apache.org.

25. JEdit is available at URL: http://www.jedit.org.

26. OpenOffice and lots of related documentation are available at the OpenOffice. org home page URL: http://www.openoffice.org/.

27. XML Spy is available from URL: http://www.xmlspy.com.

8

THE OPEN ARCHIVES INITIATIVE PROTOCOL FOR METADATA HARVESTING

Sarah L. Shreeves

The Open Archives Initiative Protocol for Metadata Harvesting (OAI-PMH) is rapidly becoming an integral part of the digital library infrastructure. From its roots in e-print archives to its inclusion in commercial digital content management systems, the OAI protocol has made significant inroads since its initial release in 2001. The purpose of this chapter is to give the nontechnical librarian a basic understanding of the protocol and its use in digital libraries. It presents fundamental information about the protocol: what it is (and is not), its history and place in the current digital library infrastructure, and how the protocol works. The chapter ends with a brief examination of some of the ongoing challenges within the OAI environment.

WHAT IS THE OAI-PMH?

Simply put, the OAI-PMH is a tool that allows metadata to be moved from one place to another. It can aid in the aggregation of descriptive metadata from disparate collections into a central data store upon which search/ retrieval and other services can be built. In this way, the OAI protocol can help provide centralized access to dispersed "hidden" resources that are not easily accessible to search engines (such as resources within databases) as well as provide a means for communities of interest to aggregate resources from different collections. The OAI protocol promotes and facilitates interoperability between dispersed collections and allows for the building of something akin to a union catalog for a wide range of resources.

Some basic definitions may be useful here. A **protocol** is a set of rules that allows communication between two systems. A well-known example is the Hypertext Transfer Protocol (HTTP) which allows HTML-encoded documents to be transferred from one machine to another and, of course, enables the World Wide Web. **Metadata** is commonly defined as "data about data." A more useful definition is "structured information about a resource" (Open Archives Forum, 2003). This information can be descriptive, structural, administrative, or technical. The machine-readable cataloging (MARC) record, which contains structured information about a bibliographic resource, is a form of descriptive metadata familiar to most librarians. **Interoperability** can be defined as the capacity of systems and organizations to work together in a seamless fashion. In the OAI context interoperability is used most often to indicate seamless discovery of and access to resources in diverse locations.

The OAI environment is divided into **data providers** who expose their repositories of metadata (not the objects the metadata describes) through the protocol, and **harvesters,** or service providers**,** who completely or selectively gather metadata from these data providers. This interaction between the data provider and the service provider is the basis of the OAI protocol. The protocol itself is based on common standards (Extensible Markup Language (XML), HTTP, and Dublin Core). A service provider sends a request to a data provider via HTTP using a specially designated **Uniform Resource Locater** (URL) called a base URL**,** along with a verb that indicates the request. The request might be for administrative information about the data provider or for all of the records in a specific metadata schema from the repository. The data provider responds to this request via HTTP with an XML record that contains the information the service provider asked for. **XML** is a language that structures and describes data. This, in a nutshell, is how the OAI protocol works. More details about the verbs and other specifics will appear later in this chapter.

The OAI protocol promotes a framework in which data providers can focus on developing collections and content and service providers can focus on building services for these collections and content. Because the OAI protocol is focused on moving the metadata—not the resources themselves—it helps to maintain a balance between institutional control and centralized access much in the way a union catalog does. Data providers maintain control over their content and allow only their metadata to be harvested via the protocol. As of July 2005 there were 674 OAI data providers from at least 33 countries (*Experimental OAI Registry*, n.d.).

While the protocol itself says nothing about what happens to metadata once harvested, usually service providers aggregate and index the harvested metadata in a central database and build search-and-retrieval and other value-added services around it. Some examples of such service providers:

- National Science Digital Library (NSDL) (http://www.nsdl.org/)
- University of Michigan's OAIster (http://oaister.umdl.umich.edu/o/oaister/)

- Emory University's AmericanSouth.org (http://www.americansouth.org/)
- Open Language Archive Community (http://www.language-archives.org/)

Brogan (2003) provides a good overview of current service providers. Figure 8.1 illustrates the relationship between data and service providers and end users.

Now that you have a brief outline of what the OAI protocol is, let us clarify what the protocol is *not*. The OAI protocol is *not* metadata (although it is often equated with Dublin Core); the protocol is a tool for moving metadata (in any format) from place to place. It is *not* a search protocol; unlike the Z39.50 protocol, the OAI protocol cannot be used to search remote databases. As you will see later, the OAI protocol does not look at the contents of a metadata record when selecting records for harvest. It is *not* a database, nor does its use mandate the use of a database. Harvesters of metadata via OAI can use the records however they wish (within the rights specified by the data provider). The OAI protocol is simply the plumbing that allows metadata to be moved from one location to another. In addition, the Open Archives Initiative should *not* be equated with the Open Access movement (a movement to promote a more open model of scholarly publishing), although OAI supports and has its roots in that community.

BACKGROUND AND PLACE IN
THE DIGITAL LIBRARY ENVIRONMENT

The OAI protocol is maintained by the Open Archives Initiative (http://www.openarchives.org/). The purpose of the Open Archives Initiative is to

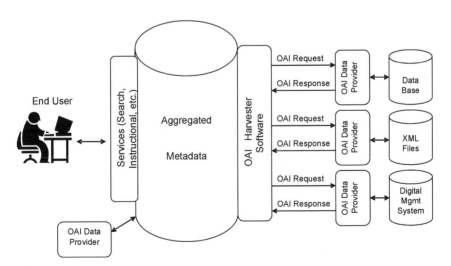

Figure 8.1 General Diagram of the OAI Environment

"develop and promote interoperability standards that aim to facilitate the efficient dissemination of content." (*Open Archives Initiative*, n.d.) The name of the initiative requires some explanation. *Open* here does not mean "free" or "unrestricted"; indeed, there are OAI data providers who share metadata only with specific service providers or who make available metadata that describes resources that are not freely accessible. The term instead indicates the promotion of a framework which promotes "machine interfaces that facilitate the availability of content from a variety of providers" (Lagoze & Van de Sompel, 2001). The term *archive* indicates only a repository of stored information, a use common in the e-prints community from which the Open Archives Initiative came. The OAI acknowledges that its use of *archive* is very different from the strict definition of the word within the library and archive tradition and asks for the "indulgence of the professional archiving community with this broader use of 'archive'" (Lagoze & Van de Sompel, 2001). The OAI maintains the technical specifications and implementation guidelines for the protocol, a registration function for data and service providers, electronic mailing lists for those interested and active in the OAI community, and extensions to the protocol and other documents. The OAI itself has an Executive Committee (made up of Herbert Van de Sompel and Carl Lagoze as of July 2004), which serves the management function, and a Technical Committee for development and evaluation of the protocol and extensions.

As already indicated, the OAI and the OAI protocol came out of the e-prints community. E-prints are electronic preprints or postprints that are usually the results of scholarly or scientific research. E-prints may range from journal articles to technical reports to dissertations (Warner, 2003). E-print archives provided a place for authors to deposit and share the results of this research in specific disciplines. Some of the better known e-print archives include arXiv (physics, computer science, and nonlinear sciences, found at http://www.arxiv.org/), Cogprints (psychology, linguistics, and neuroscience, found at http://cogprints.ecs.soton.ac.uk/, and the Networked Computer Science Technical Reference Library (NCSTRL, found athttp://www.ncstrl.org/). Much as library users often have to search multiple abstracting and indexing databases to find relevant resources, scientists and scholars had to use multiple e-print archives—each with a different interface and search technique—to be sure they found all relevant resources. In the late 1990s a group of technical experts began to look for a solution to this interoperability problem.

Two architectural frameworks offer possible solutions. The first is a broadcast or federated search approach in which remote archives (or targets) are searched in real time. The second is the harvesting approach, in which metadata is gathered from multiple archives and processed and indexed in a central database that the end user can search. Each approach has its own advantages and disadvantages. The federated search approach relies on real-time processing of end-user search queries by all targeted content providers. Librarians are generally more familiar with the Z39.50 form of federated searching. The end user receives up-to-date results in real time.

However, the federated search service is only as robust as its weakest target; that is, it is only as fast as the slowest server to which it has sent a search query. How each target has implemented the search-query language can also vary. For these and other reasons, federated search services generally do not scale well. Ranking of results from different targets can also be problematic in the federated searching approach. A harvesting approach allows a centralized service provider to aggregate, process, index, and present metadata from all content providers in a consistent manner—a similar endeavor to a union catalog. The metadata, however, is only as current as the most recent harvest; thus the end user does not get access to up-to-date results. In general, a federated search approach places the technical burden on the data provider (who must configure the search queries, etc.), while a harvesting approach places the technical burden on the service provider (Suleman & Fox, 2001). It should be noted, however, that a data provider can support both a harvesting approach and a federated search approach.

In October 1999 a group of technical experts called together by Paul Ginsparg (founder of arXiv), Rick Luce, and Herbert Van de Sompel met in Santa Fe, New Mexico, to tackle the problem of interoperability in the e-print archive community. The architectural framework chosen was based on a prototype called the Universal Preprint Service (UPS), developed by Herbert Van de Sompel, which demonstrated the potential of the harvesting model (Lagoze & Van de Sompel, 2003). The first incarnation of the OAI protocol was called the Santa Fe Convention and focused on the needs of the e-prints community (Van de Sompel & Lagoze, 2000). But the developers of the protocol quickly realized that metadata harvesting could be useful to a much wider community than simply the e-prints community. The 1.0 version of the Open Archives Initiative Protocol for Metadata Harvesting was released in January 2001 as an experimental protocol. The stable (and current) 2.0 version of the OAI protocol was released in June 2002 after extensive testing (Lagoze & Van de Sompel, 2002). For a more in-depth examination of the development of the OAI protocol see Lagoze & Van de Sompel (2003).

The hallmarks of the 2.0 version of the OAI Protocol are that it

- is "low-barrier" for data providers to implement and maintain (that is, the technical requirements are not particularly resource intensive over the long term),
- promotes the exchange of metadata about resources (not only e-prints, but anything), and
- mandates the provision of at least simple Dublin Core as a lowest common denominator metadata format for service providers to use.

In the two years since the 2.0 release the impact of the OAI protocol in the digital library world has been substantial. As noted earlier, the number of data providers using the 2.0 version of the protocol was 674 as of July 2005. These come from all types of institutions and organizations (libraries, e-print archives, academic departments, nonprofit institutions, museums, etc.) and provide access to metadata describing all types of resources (books, journals, finding aids, paintings, photographs, museum artifacts, Web pages, etc). The Andrew W. Mellon Foundation funded seven grants to explore the use of OAI in building services for scholarly communities (Waters, 2001). The core infrastructure of the NSDL is based in part on the OAI protocol (Lagoze et al., 2002). Data-provider functions are now included in open-source institutional repository products such as DSpace and Eprints.org as well as commercial content management systems such as CONTENTdm. Commercial metasearch systems such as Ex Libris' MetaLib include OAI harvesters so that libraries can include metadata from OAI data providers in their metasearch services.

The widest use of the OAI protocol is in the e-print and institutional repository communities (which are closely aligned), but other communities of interest are using the protocol as well. Two notable examples are the Open Language Archives Community (OLAC) and the Sheet Music Consortium. OLAC's mission is to create "a worldwide virtual library of language resources" through development of community-based standards for archiving and interoperability and a "network of interoperable repositories" (Open Language Archives Community, n.d.). Active in the protocol since its inception, OLAC uses the OAI protocol to create this network. It has also developed a specialized metadata schema, data-provider tools, and service-provider tools to meet the specific needs of its community (Simons & Bird, 2003). Currently, OLAC search services are hosted at the Linguist List (http://cf.linguistlist.org/) and the Language Data Consortium (http://wave.ldc.upenn.edu/). This integration of search services within key community Web sites increases the visibility and value of OLAC.

The Sheet Music Consortium (http://digital.library.ucla.edu/sheetmusic/) is a group of four academic libraries (UCLA, Johns Hopkins University, Indiana University, and Duke University) that are building an aggregation of digitized sheet music from dispersed collections. The Consortium provides standards for using unqualified Dublin Core to describe sheet music, which can be problematic to catalog because of its various parts (cover art, lyrics, musical notes, etc.) and guidelines for implementation of data-provider services (Davison, Requardt, & Brancolini, 2003). While work on this service is still in progress, the focus on building a service provider based on a specific type of material makes it an interesting model.

HOW DOES THE OAI PROTOCOL WORK?

As noted earlier, the OAI-PMH builds on other standards, notably HTTP, XML for encoding and exchanging information, and the Dublin Core

schema for metadata semantics. Service providers may request information
from data providers using a standard set of six OAI-PMH verbs. OAI-PMH
requests and responses are transmitted via HTTP (which means that you can
send OAI requests and receive responses on your Web browser). Almost all
of the OAI-PMH verbs require and/or allow the use of certain parameters
that further define the exact nature and details of the request. Data providers
process OAI-PMH requests received and reply with appropriate OAI-PMH
responses, which are always in the form of valid XML (including the metadata records themselves) and conform to top-level XML schemas defined
by the OAI protocol. An XML schema is a way to define the structure and
semantics of XML documents. The service provider can learn who the metadata provider is (that is, make an Identify request), what metadata formats it
supports (ListMetadataFormats request), and how it has divided its metadata
(ListSets request). The service provider can also request the metadata itself
(GetRecord, ListIdentifiers, and ListRecords requests). Each of these verbs
will be reviewed in more detail, but a list of the verbs and their parameters
has been provided in Table 8.1.

The OAI protocol is itself metadata neutral. That is, any (and multiple)
metadata formats can be used as long as it has a supporting XML schema to
validate against. These schemas are named within the XML document (see
Figure 8.2 for an example). However, for interoperability purposes, there is
a requirement that data providers expose metadata in simple Dublin Core.
The **Dublin Core** (DC) Metadata Element Set (or simple DC) is made up
of 15 elements maintained by the Dublin Core Metadata Initiative (DCMI)
(http://www.dublincore.org/). Its primary use is for basic resource description and discovery. The DCMI also maintains a set of qualifications to simple
DC; when used, this metadata format is often called qualified DC. Some
OAI data providers expose metadata in both simple DC and another, perhaps
more appropriate, format such as the Metadata Object Description Schema
(MODS). It should be noted that this does not necessarily require multiple
databases to store the item in each format. Because the metadata is harvested
in XML, it is possible to transform MARC XML records, for instance, into
simple DC XML records through Extensible Stylesheet Language Transformations (XSLT). XSLTs define how to transform one XML document into
another. While developing XSLTs is not easy per se, the difficult part of this
process is the intellectual mapping (or crosswalk) from one metadata format
to another.

Each item exposed through OAI is required to have a unique and persistent OAI identifier. An item is the information in a data provider's repository
from which an OAI record can be built. An item can be exposed in multiple
metadata formats. An OAI record consists of the item and its unique OAI
identifier, a date stamp, and a specific metadata format. This distinction can
be difficult to wrap your mind around. But imagine that you have a database
of items in the MODS format that you provide access to in both simple DC

and MODS via the OAI protocol. An OAI service provider will ask for a specific item in simple DC using its OAI identifier, but it can also ask for the exact same item in MODS using the same OAI identifier. The information that the service provider receives back is the OAI record. See Figures 8.3 and 8.4 for examples of the same item disseminated in two OAI records in two different metadata schemas (simple DC and MODS).

The date stamp should correspond to the date the metadata was created or last modified. Again, the distinction between the item and the OAI record is important. For instance, in the case above, if the content of an item has changed, the datestamp for the OAI record—whether in simple DC or in MODS—should reflect the modification date, because the content is different no matter what the metadata format. However, if the crosswalk from the MODS format to the simple DC format has changed, only the date stamp for the OAI records in simple DC should be updated, because only those records have changed.

Date stamps are important because they provide a way for service providers to incrementally harvest a data provider. A service provider may choose to harvest all metadata records within a repository, or it may choose to harvest records that are new or changed since a specific date. For example, the harvesting services at the University of Illinois at Urbana-Champaign (UIUC) Library conduct a full harvest once a quarter and an incremental harvest every three weeks of each data provider.

OAI VERBS

So how do the OAI verbs work? What do the requests and responses actually look like? Let's look at a typical process for a service provider. The UIUC Library maintains a service provider that focuses on aggregating cultural heritage material (the Digital Gateway to Cultural Heritage Materials, http://oai.grainger.uiuc.edu/search/). Every couple of months we look for new data providers to harvest and add to our aggregation. As yet, there is no automated way to find OAI data providers. The Open Archives Initiative maintains a list of registered OAI data providers at http://www.openarchives.org/Register/BrowseSites.pl. What is perhaps the most complete registry—compiling information from the Open Archives Initiative registry as well as other sources, including Google searches—is the Experimental OAI Registry at UIUC at http://oai.grainger.uiuc.edu/registry/. We scan and search these registries for potentially relevant data providers. When we find one that looks relevant, we typically explore it through the use of the OAI verbs. All of the OAI verbs are listed in Table 8.1.

The first OAI verb that we send is *Identify*. We can literally send this request to the data provider through a web browser. For instance, if we were interested in exploring the Library of Congress's American Memory data

Table 8.1 Verbs Used in the OAI Protocol for Metadata Harvesting

Verb Name	Purpose	Parameters	Example
Identify	Return general information about the archive and its policies (e.g., datestamp granularity)	• None	http://aerialphotos.grainger.uiuc.edu/oai.asp?verb=Identify
ListSets	Return a list of sets in which records may be organized (may be hierarchical, overlapping, or flat)	• None	http://aerialphotos.grainger.uiuc.edu/oai.asp?verb=ListSets
ListMetadata Format	List metadata formats supported by the archive as well as their schema locations and namespaces	• OAI identifier – for a specific record (Optional)	http://aerialphoto.grainger.uiuc.edu/oai.asp?verb=ListMetadat aFormats
GetRecord	Returns the metadata for a single item in the form of an OAI record	• OAI identifier (Required) • metadataPrefix – metadata format (Required) • from – start date (Optional) • until – end date (Optional) • set – set to harvest from (Optional) • resumptionToken – flow control mechanism (Exclusive)	http://aerialphotos.grainger.uiuc.edu/oai. asp?verb=GetRecord& identifier=oai:aerialphotos.grainger.uiuc.edu:AP-1A-1- 1940&metadataPrefix=oai_dc

Verb Name	Purpose	Parameters	Example
ListRecords	Returns OAI records for all items corresponding to the specified parameters	• metadataPrefix – metadata format (Required) • from – start date (Optional) • until – end date (Optional) • set – set to harvest from (Optional) • resumptionToken – flow control mechanism (Exclusive)	http://aerialphotos.grainger.uiuc.edu/oai.asp?verb=ListRecords &metadataPrefix=oai_dc
ListIdentifiers	Returns OAI headers for all items corresponding to the specified parameters	• metadataPrefix – metadata format (Required) • from – start date (Optional) • until – end date (Optional) • set – set to harvest from (Optional) • resumptionToken – flow control mechanism (Exclusive)	http://aerialphotos.grainger.uiuc.edu/oai.asps?verb=List Identifiers&metadataPrefix=oai_dc

provider, we could enter the base URL with the verb appended to it. The request looks like this:

http://memory.loc.gov/cgi-bin/oai2_0?verb=Identify

The first part of this string (before the "?") is the baseURL. The second part of this string is the OAI request. The response to an Identify request gives basic administrative information about the OAI data provider: the contact name, what version of the protocol is supported, the earliest datestamp in the repository, the granularity of the datestamp, and whether or not the repository supports deleted records. There is an optional feature in the OAI protocol that allows data providers to mark deleted records. There are also optional descriptive "containers" within the Identify response. For example, a data provider may supply a description of its repository or a link to a logo. Figure 8.2 shows you the response to the Identify request from the Library of Congress data provider.

Once we have looked at the administrative and descriptive information, we may want to determine in what formats the metadata is available. The List-MetadataFormats request asks for the metadata formats in which items (or a specific item) are available in the repository. The request looks like this:

http://memory.loc.gov/cgi-bin/oai2_0?verb=ListMetadataFormats

As noted before, in order to conform to the OAI protocol, all data providers must provide at least simple DC, which is named within the OAI protocol as 'oai_dc.'

We may also be interested in the how the data provider has structured their repository. To view this, we can issue a ListSets request, which will look like this:

http://memory.loc.gov/cgi-bin/oai2_0?verb=ListSets

Sets are an optional feature in the OAI protocol. If a data provider does not support sets, it will send a response to that effect. But if it does support sets, it will send a response that contains a list of the sets including the set name (human-readable name) and setSpec (machine-readable name) and, optionally, a description of the set. Sets are ways to organize a repository. Sets can be hierarchical, and items can belong to one or more sets. Sets provide a way for service providers to selectively harvest metadata. For example, the Sheet Music Consortium service provider might harvest only sets that contain sheet music. In practice, however, data providers have implemented sets in a number of different ways that are not always useful to service providers. Some organize their repositories based on the administrative structure of their organization. For example, an institutional repository that includes material from different departments and divisions within a university might have sets that match this structure. Other data providers have divided their

```xml
<?xml version="1.0" encoding="UTF-8" ?>
- <OAI-PMH xmlns="http://www.openarchives.org/OAI/2.0/" xmlns:xsi="http://www.w3.org/2001/XMLSchema-instance"
  xsi:schemaLocation="http://www.openarchives.org/OAI/2.0/ http://www.openarchives.org/OAI/2.0/OAI-PMH.xsd">
  <responseDate>2004-07-15T16:35:47Z</responseDate>
  <request verb="Identify">http://memory.loc.gov/cgi-bin/oai2_0</request>
- <Identify>
  <repositoryName>Library of Congress Open Archive Initiative Repository 1</repositoryName>
  <baseURL>http://memory.loc.gov/cgi-bin/oai2_0</baseURL>
  <protocolVersion>2.0</protocolVersion>
  <adminEmail>dwoo@loc.gov</adminEmail>
  <adminEmail>caar@loc.gov</adminEmail>
  <earliestDatestamp>2002-06-01T00:00:00Z</earliestDatestamp>
  <deletedRecord>no</deletedRecord>
  <granularity>YYYY-MM-DDThh:mm:ssZ</granularity>
- <description>
- <oai-identifier xmlns="http://www.openarchives.org/OAI/2.0/oai-identifier" xmlns:xsi="http://www.w3.org/2001/XMLSchema-instance"
  xsi:schemaLocation="http://www.openarchives.org/OAI/2.0/oai-identifier http://www.openarchives.org/OAI/2.0/oai-identifier.xsd">
  <scheme>oai</scheme>
  <repositoryIdentifier>lcoa1.loc.gov</repositoryIdentifier>
  <delimiter>:</delimiter>
  <sampleIdentifier>oai:lcoa1.loc.gov:loc.music/musdi.002</sampleIdentifier>
  </oai-identifier>
  </description>
- <description>
- <eprints xmlns="http://www.openarchives.org/OAI/1.1/eprints" xmlns:xsi="http://www.w3.org/2001/XMLSchema-instance"
  xsi:schemaLocation="http://www.openarchives.org/OAI/1.1/eprints http://www.openarchives.org/OAI/1.1/eprints.xsd">
- <content>
  <URL>http://memory.loc.gov/ammem/oamh/lcoa1_content.html</URL>
  <text>Selected collections of digitized historical materials from the Library of Congress, including many from American Memory. Includes photographs, movies,
     maps, pamphlets and printed ephemera, sheet music, and books.</text>
  </content>
  <metadataPolicy />
  <dataPolicy />
  </eprints>
  </description>
- <description>
- <branding xmlns="http://www.openarchives.org/OAI/2.0/branding/" xmlns:xsi="http://www.w3.org/2001/XMLSchema-instance"
  xsi:schemaLocation="http://www.openarchives.org/OAI/2.0/branding/ http://www.openarchives.org/OAI/2.0/branding.xsd">
- <collection.icon>
  <url>http://memory.loc.gov/ammem/oamh/lc-icon.gif</url>
  <link>http://www.loc.gov</link>
  <title>Library of Congress</title>
  <width>100</width>
  <height>35</height>
  </collection.icon>
  <metadataRendering metadataNamespace="http://www.loc.gov/MARC21/slim"
  mimeType="text/xsl">http://www.loc.gov/standards/marcxml/xslt/MARC21slim2HTML.xsl</metadataRendering>
  </branding>
  </description>
  </Identify>
  </OAI-PMH>
```

Figure 8.2 Response to an "Identify" Request

repositories based on defined collections, format of material, or whether the resources described are free or restricted.

While designed to be machine-to-machine understandable, these first three verbs (Identify, ListMetadataFormats, and ListSets) typically need some sort of human interpretation. We need to read the descriptive information provided in responses to determine whether we are interested in harvesting this data provider. Once we have established our interest in the data provider, we typically run automated processes to harvest the metadata using special software programs called harvesters. The remaining three verbs (GetRecord, ListRecords and ListIdentifiers) can be used for this purpose. The harvesters send these OAI requests and capture the information contained within the OAI response. Once captured, the information might be stored as XML files or within a database, or both.

If we are interested in a specific item within the data provider's repository we might issue a GetRecord request. A GetRecord request is required to include the OAI identifier of the record as well as the specific metadata format we are interested in (using the *metadataPrefix* parameter). A GetRecord request looks like this:

http://memory.loc.gov/cgi-bin/oai2_0?verb=GetRecord&metadataPrefix=oai_
dc&identifier=oai%3Alcoa1.loc.gov%3Aloc.pnp%2Fcwpbh.00004

Figure 8.3 shows the response to this request. Note that the response echoes back the OAI request. The next section of the response is the <header> container which includes the OAI identifier, the date stamp, and setSpecs (i.e., the sets to which the item belongs). After the <header> is the <metadata> container. This contains a reference to the XML schema in use for the metadata format as well as the metadata itself.

Figure 8.4 shows the response to a GetRecord request for the same item, but in the MODS metadata schema. This GetRecord request looks like this:

http://memory.loc.gov/cgi-bin/oai2_0?verb=GetRecord&metadataPrefix=mods&
identifier=oai%3Alcoa1.loc.gov%3Aloc.pnp%2Fcwpbh.00004

Note that the content of the metadata is the same but in a different metadata format. The date stamp could potentially be different, but in this case it is the same.

There is an optional container that can also be included with an OAI record: the <about> container. The <about> container, if used, typically holds information about the provenance or rights associated with the metadata. Each <about> container can only include one type of information (provenance or rights) but can be repeated as many times as necessary. Provenance information allows data providers to identify the origin of each metadata record. This is especially important because service providers can (and do) make their aggregation available via the OAI protocol (as illustrated in Figure 8.1).

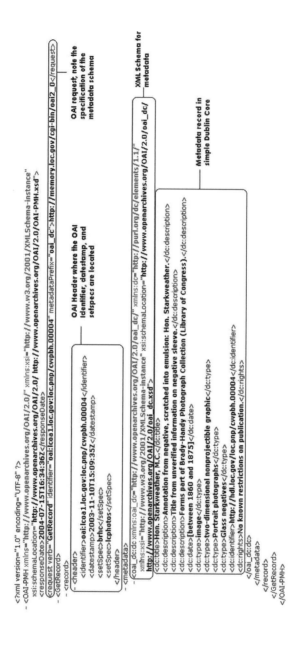

```
<?xml version="1.0" encoding="UTF-8" ?>
- <OAI-PMH xmlns="http://www.openarchives.org/OAI/2.0/" xmlns:xsi="http://www.w3.org/2001/XMLSchema-instance"
  xsi:schemaLocation="http://www.openarchives.org/OAI/2.0/ http://www.openarchives.org/OAI/2.0/OAI-PMH.xsd">
  <responseDate>2004-07-15T16:34:36Z</responseDate>
  <request verb="GetRecord" identifier="oai:lcoa1.loc.gov:loc.pnp/cwpbh.00004" metadataPrefix="oai_dc">http://memory.loc.gov/cgi-bin/oai2_0</request>
- <GetRecord>
  - <record>
    - <header>
        <identifier>oai:lcoa1.loc.gov:loc.pnp/cwpbh.00004</identifier>
        <datestamp>2003-11-10T15:09:35Z</datestamp>
        <setSpec>brhc</setSpec>
        <setSpec>lcphotos</setSpec>
      </header>
    - <metadata>
      - <oai_dc:dc xmlns:oai_dc="http://www.openarchives.org/OAI/2.0/oai_dc/" xmlns:dc="http://purl.org/dc/elements/1.1/"
        xmlns:xsi="http://www.w3.org/2001/XMLSchema-instance" xsi:schemaLocation="http://www.openarchives.org/OAI/2.0/oai_dc/
        http://www.openarchives.org/OAI/2.0/oai_dc.xsd">
          <dc:title>Hon. Starkweather, M.C.</dc:title>
          <dc:description>Annotation from negative, scratched into emulsion: Hon. Starkweather.</dc:description>
          <dc:description>Title from unverified information on negative sleeve.</dc:description>
          <dc:description>Forms part of Brady-Handy Photograph Collection (Library of Congress).</dc:description>
          <dc:date>[between 1860 and 1875]</dc:date>
          <dc:type>image</dc:type>
          <dc:type>two-dimensional nonprojectible graphic</dc:type>
          <dc:type>Portrait photographs</dc:type>
          <dc:type>Glass negatives</dc:type>
          <dc:identifier>http://hdl.loc.gov/loc.pnp/cwpbh.00004</dc:identifier>
          <dc:rights>No known restrictions on publication.</dc:rights>
        </oai_dc:dc>
      </metadata>
    </record>
  </GetRecord>
</OAI-PMH>
```

OAI request; note the specification of the metadata schema

OAI Header where the OAI Identifier, datestamp, and setspecs are located

XML Schema for metadata

Metadata record in simple Dublin Core

Figure 8.3 Response to a "GetRecord" Request in Simple Dublin Core

98

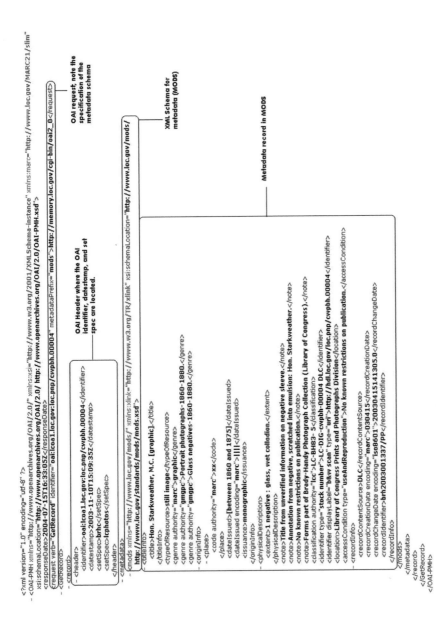

```
<?xml version="1.0" encoding="utf-8" ?>
- <OAI-PMH xmlns="http://www.openarchives.org/OAI/2.0/" xmlns:xsi="http://www.w3.org/2001/XMLSchema-instance" xmlns:marc="http://www.loc.gov/MARC21/slim"
    xsi:schemaLocation="http://www.openarchives.org/OAI/2.0/ http://www.openarchives.org/OAI/2.0/OAI-PMH.xsd">
  <responseDate>2004-07-15T16:33:05Z</responseDate>
  <request verb="GetRecord" identifier="oai:lcoa1.loc.gov:loc.pnp/cwpbh.00004" metadataPrefix="mods">http://memory.loc.gov/cgi-bin/oai2_0</request>
- <GetRecord>
 - <record>
  - <header>
     <identifier>oai:lcoa1.loc.gov:loc.pnp/cwpbh.00004</identifier>
     <datestamp>2003-11-10T15:09:35Z</datestamp>
     <setSpec>brhc</setSpec>
     <setSpec>lcphotos</setSpec>
   </header>
 - <metadata>
 - <mods xmlns="http://www.loc.gov/mods/" xmlns:xlink="http://www.w3.org/TR/xlink" xsi:schemaLocation="http://www.loc.gov/mods/
   http://www.loc.gov/standards/mods/mods.xsd">
  - <titleInfo>
     <title>Hon. Starkweather, M.C. [graphic].</title>
   </titleInfo>
     <typeOfResource>still image</typeOfResource>
     <genre authority="marc">graphic</genre>
     <genre authority="gmgpc">Portrait photographs-1860-1880.</genre>
     <genre authority="gmgpc">Glass negatives-1860-1880.</genre>
  - <originInfo>
   - <place>
       <code authority="marc">xx</code>
     </place>
     <dateIssued>[between 1860 and 1875]</dateIssued>
     <dateIssued encoding="marc">llll</dateIssued>
     <issuance>monographic</issuance>
   </originInfo>
  - <physicalDescription>
     <extent>1 negative : glass, wet collodion.</extent>
   </physicalDescription>
     <note>Title from unverified information on negative sleeve.</note>
     <note>Annotation from negative, scratched into emulsion: Hon. Starkweather.</note>
     <note>No known restrictions on publication.</note>
     <note>Forms part of Brady-Handy Photograph Collection (Library of Congress).</note>
     <classification authority="lcc">LC-BH83-5</classification>
     <identifier type="stock number">LC-DIG-cwpbh-00004 DLC</identifier>
     <identifier displayLabel="b&w scan" type="uri">http://hdl.loc.gov/loc.pnp/cwpbh.00004</identifier>
     <location>Library of Congress Prints and Photographs Division</location>
     <accessCondition type="useAndReproduction">No known restrictions on publication.</accessCondition>
   - <recordInfo>
       <recordContentSource>DLC</recordContentSource>
       <recordCreationDate encoding="marc">030415</recordCreationDate>
       <recordChangeDate encoding="iso8601">20030415141305.0</recordChangeDate>
       <recordIdentifier>brh2003001337/PP</recordIdentifier>
     </recordInfo>
   </mods>
 </metadata>
</record>
</GetRecord>
</OAI-PMH>
```

OAI request; note the specification of the metadata schema

OAI Header where the OAI identifier, datestamp, and set spec are located.

XML Schema for metadata (MODS)

Metadata record in MODS

Figure 8.4 Response to a "GetRecord" Request in MODS

99

Because the items in an aggregation were created elsewhere, service providers should (but are not required to) ensure that the provenance information is included in the <about> container along with the metadata so that the harvester knows where the item originated.

An <about> container can also include rights information. This is a place to record statements about intellectual-property rights associated with the metadata. The rights statement within the <about> container is *not* applicable to the resource the metadata describes; that should be within the metadata itself. Again, service providers should (but are not required to) respect the rights specified within the <about> container. This may mean that a service provider cannot modify a metadata record—a common practice among service providers. A group within the Open Archives Initiative is currently working on an implementation guideline on how rights information should be conveyed within an OAI record.

If we want all of the records in a repository we can use the ListRecords request. Again, we have to indicate which metadata format we want the records in, using the *metadataPrefix* parameter. We could also limit the records to those in a specific set, using the *setSpec* parameter. In addition we could limit the records to those added or modified within a specific date range, using the *from* and *until* parameters for a specific set or for the entire repository. A ListRecords request looks like this:

http://memory.loc.gov/cgi-bin/oai2_0?verb=ListRecords&metadataPrefix=oai_dc

The request above asks the Library of Congress to list all of their records within their repository. The Library of Congress is a large data provider. As of July 2005, it contained 198,047 records. Sending an XML file that contains all of these files can place a large processing load on the server. The OAI protocol includes an optional feature called a resumptionToken. A resumptionToken is a way for data providers to establish flow control; that is, they can control the size of the XML file that is sent to harvesters. If we ask the Library of Congress for all of their records, they may respond with one XML file containing 100 OAI records and at the end of the file a resumptionToken. A harvester will issue a second ListRecords request that includes the *resumptionToken* parameter; for instance:

http://memory.loc.gov/cgi-bin/oai2_0?verb=ListRecords&resumptionToken=eQ
aD

The Library of Congress will respond with the next 100 records and a new resumptionToken. This will proceed until all of the records are harvested.

The last OAI request is ListIdentifiers. Again, you must indicate which metadata schema you are interested in, using the *metadataPrefix* parameter. As with the ListRecords request, you can also specify a specific date range, using the *from* and *until* parameter, and/or a specific set, using the *setSpec* parameter. Also, a data provider may institute flow control for this request using the *resumptionToken*. A ListIdentifiers request might look like this:

http://memory.loc.gov/cgi-bin/oai2_0?verb=ListIdentifiers&metadataPrefix=oai _dc

The response to this request contains only the information in the <header> container that we saw in Figures 8.3 and 8.4. Some harvesting programs use the ListIdentifiers request to harvest data providers record by record. The program records each of the OAI identifiers listed in the response, and then issues a GetRecord request for each one. This harvesting method is a good option for data providers who have not implemented the resumptionToken feature and have a large number of records within their repository as it places much less strain on the server than a ListRecords request.

The section above outlined the basics of how the OAI protocol works. To learn more details, there are a number of resources available on the World Wide Web:

- The Open Archives Initiative Protocol for Metadata Harvesting, Version 2.0 (http://www.openarchives.org/OAI_protocol/openarchivesprotocol.html)
- Implementation Guidelines for the Open Archives Initiative Protocol for Metadata Harvesting (http://www.openarchives.org/OAI/2.0/guidelines.htm)
- OAI for Beginners, the Open Archives Forum Online Tutorial (http://www. oaforum.org/tutorial/)

The remainder of this chapter will briefly cover the challenges that the OAI community faces, in particular the challenges that service providers face when aggregating metadata from diverse sources.

CHALLENGES FOR THE OAI COMMUNITY

As the OAI protocol has become more widely adopted, some broad areas of concern have surfaced—mainly through the documentation of service providers. Some of these concerns center on technical issues related to how data-provider services have been implemented—in particular use or nonuse of certain optional features. For example, use of set description would allow service providers to easily determine the types of materials within sets and whether to harvest them. There is an effort within the Digital Library Federation to establish guidelines and best practices for OAI data provider implementations.

A less tractable issue is the metadata itself. The range of OAI data providers, the types of resources they describe, and how they describe them can present a fundamental challenge to service providers as they try to build effective search and browse functions for aggregated metadata. This is particularly true for service providers who are capturing metadata from a large range of data providers.

There are important differences in how certain communities may decide to describe their resources. As a broad generalization, libraries are typically concerned with access; archives, with preserving context; and museums, with providing interpretation. These concerns will affect how these organizations describe their material in terms of which metadata formats are used, which controlled vocabularies and encoding schemes are used, and how deeply items are described. In particular, the use of disparate controlled vocabularies (not to mention the use of keywords) in the subject element in simple DC makes the provision of browse functions particularly difficult. This difficulty is compounded because in simple DC there is not a place to indicate which controlled vocabulary is in use.

The problems associated with aggregating metadata have been well documented (Arms et al., 2003; Halbert, 2003; Hagedorn, 2003; Shreeves, Kaczmarek, & Cole, 2003), but one of the most significant problems is information loss.

Information loss can occur in at least two ways. The first is when data providers map from complex metadata formats to simple DC. The semantics of simple DC are not able to express, for instance, the difference between a date a book was published and the date it was digitized. In many cases this information existed in the original native metadata format. However, most data providers expose only simple DC via OAI despite the protocol's ability to handle multiple metadata formats. There are several reasons for this. In some cases the data provider is using a turnkey system (such as a commercial content management system), which provides only basic OAI data provider functionality and does not allow the export of multiple metadata formats. In other cases, an XML schema does not exist for the native metadata format, and the data provider does not have the technical expertise to write one. And, finally, some data providers are simply not aware that they are able to expose multiple metadata formats via the OAI protocol.

Information loss can also occur when metadata is taken out of its local context. Most metadata is written for use by a well-understood local audience and for a specific context. For example, Figure 8.5 is a screenshot of a metadata record from the Teaching with Digital Content collection based at the UIUC. The purpose of this collection is to provide access to items in museums and libraries that could be used in the curriculum of teachers in Illinois. The metadata includes the state learning standard and particular lesson plans (available elsewhere on the site) to be used in conjunction with the item. Figure 8.6 is the record as it appears in the Digital Gateway to Cultural Heritage Resources at UIUC. The combination of taking the record out of its local context and mapping it to simple DC has compounded the information loss The learning standard "16 History" no longer has any meaning.

Title: Letter from Abraham Lincoln to Jesse K. Dubois

Coverage / Year: August 19, 1856

Description: Letter from Abraham Lincoln to Jesse K. Dubois, one of Lincoln's neighbors in Springfield, concerning the presidential election. DuBois served with Lincoln as Whig in the Illinois General Assembly, and in 1865, Lincoln recommended DuBois for Illinois State Auditor, a position he held for eight years. This letter was given to the University of Illinois as a gift of Leonora H. Watts, a 1919 University of Illinois graduate, who specified that it be placed in the Sandburg Collection. The letter reads: Springfield, Aug. 19, 1856 Dear Dubois: Your letter on the same sheet with Mr. Miller's is just received. I have been absent four days. I do not know when your court sits. Trumbull has written the Committee here to have a set of appointments made for him commencing here in Springfield, on the 11th of Sept., and to extend throughout the south half of the State. When he goes to Lawrenceville, as he will, I will strain every nerve to be with you and him. More than that I cannot promise now. Yours as truly as ever, A. Lincoln. (Text copied from The Collected Works of Abraham Lincoln, II, p.360, R.P. Basler, Editor, M.D. Pratt & L.A. Dunlap, Assistant Editors, Rutgers UP, NJ, 1953).

Interpretation: In this letter to one of his Springfield neighbors, Lincoln promises to return from Washington whenever he can to be of service to help support the new Republican Party and its presidential nominee, John C. Fremont. Though Fremont was defeated by James Buchanan, the new Republican Party scored significant victories in Illinois.

Lesson Plans / Themes: Governing Ourselves
Government in Illinois
Choosing the Lincoln Statue
Antebellum Society and the Civil War

Learning Standards: 16 History
14 Political Systems

Author or Creator: Lincoln, Abraham, 1809-1865

Collection Publisher: UIUC Rare Book & Special Collections Library

Subject / Keywords: Lincoln, Abraham, 1809-1865
Dubois, Jesse K.

Rights Management Statement: http://images.library.uiuc.edu/projects/tdc/conditions.htm

Resource Identifier: conncoll468

Figure 8.5 Metadata for "Letter from Abraham Lincoln to Jesse K. Dubois"—Native Format

```xml
<?xml version="1.0" encoding="iso-8859-1" ?>
- <rss version="2.0" xmlns:admin="http://purl.org/dc/elements/1.1/" xmlns:sy="http://purl.org/rss/1.0/modules/syndication/" xmlns:admin="http://webns.net/mvcb/" xmlns:rdf="http://www.w3.org/1999/02/22-rdf-syntax-ns#" xmlns:content="http://purl.org/rss/1.0/modules/content/">
  - <channel>
    <title>In the Spotlight</title>
    <link>http://www.library.northwestern.edu/news/</link>
    <description>News from Northwestern University Library</description>
    <dc:language>en-us</dc:language>
    <dc:creator>p-strait@northwestern.edu</dc:creator>
    <dc:date>2004-07-16T13:47:51-06:00</dc:date>
    <admin:generatorAgent rdf:resource="http://www.movabletype.org/?v=2.63" />
    <sy:updatePeriod>hourly</sy:updatePeriod>
    <sy:updateFrequency>1</sy:updateFrequency>
    <sy:updateBase>2000-01-01T12:00+00:00</sy:updateBase>
    - <item>
      <title>Children's book illustrations on exhibit</title>
      <link>http://www.library.northwestern.edu/news/archives/000485.html</link>
      <description>O Gato e O Escuro (The Cat and the Dark) illustrated by Danuta Wojciechowska and written by Mia Couto (Editorial Caminho, 2001, 2003)Orange cats jumping over a dark moon. A cool fish waving a top hat. A kindhearted monster...</description>
      - <content:encoded>
      - <![CDATA[
        <p><img alt="gato2.jpg" src="http://www.library.northwestern.edu/news/archives/gato2.jpg" width="250" height="290" border="0" /><br />
        <b><p class="caption"><i>O Gato e O Escuro </i>(The Cat and the Dark) illustrated by Danuta Wojciechowska and

        <p>The lively work of childrenⅡs book illustrators from around the world will be on display at Northwestern U

        <p>The Hans Christian Andersen Awards are presented every two years by the International Board on Books for Y

        <p>Jeffrey Garrett of Northwestern University Library served as president of the 2004 Hans Christian Andersen
```

Figure 8.6 Metadata for "Letter from Abraham Lincoln to Jesse K. Dubois"—Dublin Core

Another example of information loss is what Robin Wendler, metadata analyst at Harvard University Library, has termed the "on a horse" problem (Wendler, 2004). If you have a collection of digitized material that is all about Mark Twain, your metadata may not include the subject heading "Mark Twain" or "Samuel Clemens" because it is obvious that everything in the database is about Mark Twain. But when this metadata is made available via the OAI protocol, it no longer has its original environment to provide that basic concept. Wendler's descriptive term comes from a collection about Theodore Roosevelt that has this problem. Photographs of Roosevelt on a horse simple had the singularly nonuseful (out of its local context, at least!) descriptive entry "On a horse."

Information loss in all of these situations can be mitigated through several methods:

- Provision of the native metadata format in addition to simple DC via the OAI protocol
- Inclusion in the simple DC records of the semantics of the more complex metadata format; for example, <date>published: 1838</date> or <description>Illinois learning standard: 15 History</description>
- Careful attention and consideration to interoperability during the metadata creation process
- Provision of collection-level metadata to give contextual information for item level material
- Communication between data and service providers to better understand the context and semantics of metadata records

The problems presented by metadata aggregation and the suggested strategies for handling them emphasize an important tension that underlies the OAI model as a whole: what data providers are responsible for versus what service providers are responsible for. While the OAI protocol itself is relatively simple or low barrier for data providers to implement and for service providers to use (setting up a service provider is a more technically intensive process), working with the metadata itself is proving to be more difficult. Service providers can and do process and change aggregated metadata to provide normalized values for certain fields and to augment metadata to provide additional context. Data providers need to also pay careful attention to the metadata they are exposing via the OAI protocol to ensure that it is useful for service providers. Efforts from both players in the OAI environment will help ensure that the OAI protocol and harvesting model remains a useful tool and framework for interoperable access to dispersed collections.

CONCLUSION

This chapter has really only touched the surface of what could be said about the OAI protocol. This chapter did not enumerate the numerous

Open Source software tools available for OAI data providers (see the Open Archives Initiative Web site for a list of tools) nor what typical data-provider implementations look like. There are numerous other metadata-aggregation issues other than those outlined above, and the OAI protocol has begun to be used in ways other than for metadata transfer (Van de Sompel, 2003).

REFERENCES

The references below and the ones included within the chapter are useful resources for more information about the OAI protocol and metadata aggregation.

Arms, W. Y., Dushay, N., Fulker, D., and Lagoze, C. (2003). A case study in metadata harvesting: the NSDL. *Library Hi Tech, 21*(2), 228–237.

Brogan, M. (2003). A survey of digital library aggregation services. Washington, D.C.: Digital Library Federation. URL: http://www.diglib.org/pubs/ brogan/ (Accessed June 2, 2004).

Davis, J. R., and Lagoze, C. (2000). NCSTRL: Design and deployment of a globally distributed digital library. *Journal of the American Society for Information Science, 51*(3), 273–280.

Davison, S., Requardt., C., and Brancolini, K. (2003). A Specialized Open Archives Initiative Harvester for Sheet Music: A Project Report and Examination of Issues. Paper presented at the Fourth International Conference on Music Information Retrieval: October 26–30, 2003, Baltimore, Maryland, USA. URL: http://ismir2003.ismir.net/papers/Davison.PDF. (Accessed June 2, 2004).

Experimental OAI Registry at UIUC. (n.d.). URL: http://oai.grainger.uiuc.edu/ registry/ (Accessed July 6, 2004).

Hagedorn, K. (2003). "OAIster: A 'no dead ends' OAI service provider." *Library Hi Tech, 21*(2), 170–181.

Halbert, M. (2003). The Metascholar Initiative: AmericanSouth.Org and Meta Archive.Org. *Library Hi Tech, 21*(2), 182–198.

Lagoze, C., and Van de Sompel, H. (2001). The open archives initiative: building a low-barrier interoperability framework. In E. A. Fox and C. L. Borgman (Eds.), *Proceedings of First ACM/IEEE-CS Joint Conference on Digital Libraries: June 24–28, 2001: Roanoke, Virginia, USA* (pp. 54–62). New York: ACM Press.

Lagoze, C., and Van de Sompel, H. (2002). *The open archives initiative protocol for metadata harvesting – version 2.0.* URL: http://www.openarchives.org/OAI_ protocol/openarchivesprotocol.html. (Accessed June 2, 2004).

Lagoze, C., and Van de Sompel, H. (2003). The making of the open archives initiative protocol for metadata harvesting. *Library Hi Tech, 21*(2), 118–128.

Lagoze, C., Hoehn, W., Millman, D., Arms, W., Gan, S., Hillmann, D., Ingram, C., Kraft, D., Marisa, R., Phipps, J., Saylor, J., Terrizzi, C., Allan, J., Guzman-Lara, S., and Kait, T. (2002). Core services in the architecture of the National Science Digital Library (NSDL). In G. Marchionini and W. R. Hersh (Eds.),

Proceedings of the Second ACM/IEEE-CS Joint Conference on Digital Libraries: July 14–18, 2002, Portland, Oregon (pp. 201–209). New York: ACM Press.

Lagoze, C., Van de Sompel, H., Nelson, M., and Warner, S. (2002). *Implementation guidelines for the open archives initiative protocol for metadata harvesting.* URL: http://www.openarchives.org/OAI/2.0/guidelines.htm. (Accessed June 2, 2004).

Open Archives Forum. (2003). *OAI for beginners: The open archives forum online tutorial.* URL: http://www.oaforum.org/tutorial/ (Accessed June 2, 2004).

Open Archives Initiative. (n.d.) URL: http://www.openarchives.org/ (Accessed June 2, 2004).

Open Language Archives Community. (n.d.) URL: http://www.language-archives.org/ (Accessed June 2, 2004).

Shreeves, S. L., Kaczmarek, J., and Cole, T. W. (2003). Harvesting cultural heritage metadata using the OAI protocol. *Library Hi Tech, 21*(2), 159–169.

Simons, G. and Bird, S. (2003). Building an Open Language Archives community on the OAI foundation. *Library Hi Tech, 21*(2), 210–218.

Suleman, H., and Fox, E. (2001). The Open Archives Initiative: Realizing Simple and Effective Digital Library Interoperability. *Journal of Library Administration, 35*(1/2), 125–145.

Van de Sompel, H., and Lagoze, C. (2000). The Santa Fe convention of the open archives initiative. *D-Lib Magazine, 6*(2). URL: http://www.dlib.org/dlib/february00/vandesompel-oai/02vandesompel-oai.html. (Accessed July 6, 2004).

Van de Sompel, H., Young, J.A., and Hickey, T.B. (2003). Using the OAI-PMH... differently. *D-Lib Magazine, 9*(7/8). URL: http://www.dlib.org/dlib/july03/young/07young.html (Accessed June 3, 2004).

Warner, S. (2003). E-prints and the open archives initiative. *Library Hi Tech, 21*(2), 151–158.

Waters, D. (2001). The metadata harvesting initiative of the Mellon Foundation. *ARL Bimonthly Report, 217.* URL: http://www.arl.org/newsltr/217/waters. (Accessed June 3, 2004).

Wendler, R. (2004). The eye of the beholder: Challenges of image description and access at Harvard. In Diane Hillmann and Elaine Westbrooks (Eds.), *Metadata in Practice.* Chicago: ALA Editions.

9

---·•··—

INSTITUTIONAL REPOSITORIES

Charly Bauer

Many universities and colleges around the world have built institutional repositories to begin capturing and preserving their scholarly digital content. Many others have embraced the idea and are making plans of their own. Others are just beginning to explore the potential for an institutional repository at their campus and are seeking more information.

The purpose of this chapter is to

- describe in nontechnical terms the key features and functions of institutional repositories and the software that is available to build them and
- provide details of the OhioLINK library consortium's statewide system, which will provide hosted institutional repository services for the state.

This article attempts to delve into topics that were introduced in a presentation by MacKenzie Smith, MIT Libraries, and myself at the May 27, 2004, seminar, "Technology for the Rest of Us: What Every Librarian Should Understand about the Technologies that Affect Us."

It is intended for academic librarians interested in planning and preparing for an institutional repository at their institution. It will provide useful background information and hopefully encourage creative thinking about how to provide collaborative, multi-institutional services.

WHAT IS AN INSTITUTIONAL REPOSITORY?

Clifford Lynch provides a useful working definition of an institutional repository (IR): "a set of services that a university offers to the members of its community for the management and dissemination of digital materials created by the institution and its community members" (Lynch, 2003, p. 328).

IRs should be considered as part of the open-access movement, specifically open-access self-archiving. In open-access self-archiving, a research paper is first published in a traditional academic journal, for example. The author, with permission from the publisher, then publishes the article on his institution's Web site, or on a discipline-specific site devoted to the same type of content. The publisher may provide restrictions such as a time period before which the self-archiving may begin or limits on which version of the paper may be self-archived.

IR use in practice now includes a greater breadth of content. The types of materials might include faculty research (articles, presentations, data sets, preprints or postprints, and so forth), student theses and dissertations, teaching materials (including so-called Learning Objects, i.e. digital resources that can be reused to support learning), archival materials, image collections, and just about anything that is or can be made digital and relates to the function of the university. Typically, preservation is another aim of the repository.

An IR usually manifests itself as a Web page that provides a single point of access to institutionally created content. The most common items found are Adobe PDF files of research papers, though other content formats and digital file types are emerging. Usually, simple and advanced searching is offered as is browsing by collection, date, author, and title. It is possible to imagine a small-scale IR not offering search services.

A must-read document on IRs is "The Case for Institutional Repositories: A SPARC Position Paper" (Crow, 2002). Two rationales for repositories are presented. First, that repositories can facilitate a shift in scholarly publishing by eliminating the problems of high price and limited access, and second, that they can enhance institutional prestige and visibility by highlighting its output.

A list of related readings and information is provided at the end of this chapter.

WHY SHOULD LIBRARIES BE INVOLVED?

It is important to ask why the library should play any role in this effort. Should someone else on campus handle this instead? Perhaps a campus computing department, the Chief Information Officer's office, or individual academic departments or colleges should be responsible? Libraries should be involved because they already serve as stewards of content.

The library possesses unique expertise and experience in areas critical to the success of IRs:

• Organization, access, and sharing
• Preservation

- Standardization
- Cross-institutional service

The library should not be the *only* player in the development of IRs. Rather, close collaboration with academic units and campus information-technology departments is critical to the success of such a project. But the library should take on the role of stewards of this type of information as it has with traditional published information that it purchases.

What's Going on at My Campus?

You should determine who on campus is already posting the type of information you intend to host in your IR. It will be useful to determine who is already making faculty research (and other types of institutionally created works) available online from your own institution. Try using your institutional Web site's search function (or Google or another search engine) to determine if there are research articles in PDF form available online already. In Google, for instance, type "effects site:myuniversity.edu filetype:pdf" into the search box, making sure to replace "myuniversity.edu" with your institution's domain name. This should return PDF articles with the word "effects" in the title or in the text that have been posted on your institution's Web site. The "effects" keyword tends to provide a good place to start and good results, because it is often used in research papers, although plenty of other words would work well too. Likewise you should also try searching for other file formats, such as .doc.

Unless there is a mistake or confusion, the articles you find are intended for broad consumption on the Internet. They were likely posted by the author and with the author's consent. They are intended to be available to a wide audience.

The quantity of articles returned may help you focus your efforts to build an IR. If there are many articles already available online, your marketing and development efforts will be easier. In that case you will not need to convince authors that putting research output online is important—rather you will need to convince them that putting works online in the IR is a more useful solution than what they are currently doing. If you find few articles, you will need to focus your efforts on how to get more articles online while simultaneously convincing authors that the IR should be the location of choice.

You should select a few of the works you find online and research their status and provenance.

- Who authored the work?
- On what Web site is the article hosted? Through what department, center, other?
- Is the unit that hosts the Web site/article providing any search engine or other access mechanisms?

- Is the unit that hosts the Web site and article publishing metadata that can be harvested?
- Is the unit that hosts the Web site committed to preserving the article and migrating the format if necessary?
- Is the article integrated with other, similar resources?
- What other units are also posting articles? Are they doing redundant work on campus? Is it effective?

The answers to these questions can form the basis for your case to build an IR and the service agreements you will choose to implement. They may also provide direction for your marketing strategy as you position the IR on campus.

How Will My IR Benefit Our Community?

In order to build an IR that materially benefits the author and the institution, it should provide the following:

- *Mission-critical availability.* Like the online public access catalog (OPAC), the IR should be treated as a mission-critical resource that requires regular data backups and technical solutions that minimize disruption. Service agreements secure maximum availability and integrity.
- *Maximum exposure and accessibility.* Libraries can add value to content by creating catalog records or metadata for submitted items. The purpose of this is both local access and allowing the metadata to be made available in global registries of academic resources of this type. This metadata should be in a recognized standard and should be made available via the Open Archives Initiative (OAI) protocol.
- *Preservation.* Libraries are the long-term caretakers of content on their campus. This commitment to preservation should extend to the materials in the IR. This distinguishes the IR from other campus-based Web sites.

Who's Doing What with IRs?

There are several important IR projects worth investigating before you begin planning or building your own.

DSpace at MIT

Anyone who begins an IR service should start by looking at DSpace (https://dspace.mit.edu). DSpace is many things, one of which is an IR, a service provided by the Massachusetts Institute of Technology (MIT) Libraries for the MIT research community. DSpace is also the name of the open source software behind the service. The software platform itself is discussed in a later section. (This is somewhat confusing, like having your library OPAC named after its vendor or product name).

Content in DSpace is organized, or grouped, into "Community and Collection." A community is a scholarly unit such as a center, institutes, academic department, or university press. This seems to be a widely used organizational structure for IRs. It is a useful way to market an IR service on a campus. It will be more efficient to solicit groups of like-minded faculty members at once rather than issuing an open call for participation across campus. Collections are arbitrary groupings of items. These collections could include, for example, annual proceedings, or a series of papers on a specific issue.

DSpace at MIT contains nearly 4,000 submitted items, including preprints, conference papers, and technical reports, as well as images from 10 different communities. Items are presented in a single interface that supports searching across the entire DSpace service or within a specific community or collection. Browsing by community, collection, author, title, or date is also supported.

EScholarship Repository at the University of California System

The California Digital Library sponsors the eScholarship Repository (http://repositories.cdlib.org/escholarship). This is a central service that hosts research materials from scholars in the University of California system.

Like MIT's DSpace, the eScholarship Repository is organized around communities such as research units, centers, or academic departments. Each community is identified with logos and other customized interfaces as necessary.

eScholarship is multi-institutional and centralized. It is a service that provides institutional repository functionality for participants but is hosted and administered from a single site rather than at multiple locations. This reduces infrastructure redundancy, thereby reducing costs.

The service also supports digital publishing activities for journals and peer-reviewed series. For example, the journal *InterActions: UCLA Journal of Education and Information Studies* is published through the eScholarship Repository.

More than 3,000 papers are stored in the repository. Associated content such as spreadsheets, presentations, or images may be provided along with papers. Searching and browsing functions are offered.

Caltech Collection of Open Digital Archives

The California Institute of Technology (Caltech) has built the Caltech Collection of Open Digital Archives (CODA) system (http://library.caltech.edu/digital/). The content the system supports includes books, theses and dissertations, oral histories, technical reports, and research papers.

Hong Kong University of Science and Technology

There are 1,406 items in the Hong Kong University of Science and Technology's Institutional Repository (HKUST). HKUST uses DSpace software, and thus the look and feel and functionality of its system is very similar to DSpace at MIT.

Other Institutional Repositories

SPARC (http://www.arl.org/sparc/core/index.asp?page=m1) maintains a directory of IRs around the world, organized by country. The site describes the technology each institution uses to build its system.

A SUCCESSFUL IR

Marketing the IR

Marketing of your IR is critical. First you must market the service to the librarians on campus. Librarians should form the front line of the effort to gain broad acceptance across campus. They should be educated as to the purpose and benefits of the IR for the broader campus community, and they should embrace the concept and goals of the repository. Without the acceptance of the librarians first, it will be even more difficult to achieve broader acceptance by the faculty.

After you market internally to the library community, marketing to the faculty becomes the next challenge. You may experience indifference, confusion, or outright rejection. It is likely that the response will vary by academic department. Some groups may already be familiar with the concept, while it may be completely new for others. Be aware that some researchers at your institution may already be using discipline-specific archives, especially researchers in the sciences. The discipline-specific archives available include Cogprints, PubMedCentral, PhilSci Archive, and arXiv. You should determine early how you will position your institutional archive in relation to them.

Now that many repository services have moved from development into the operational stage, institutions are starting to focus on techniques and strategies for marketing and achieving growth in the use of the service. We should start to see more publications, conferences, and training opportunities that directly address marketing and growth strategies for IRs.

Copyright and Intellectual Property Issues

Copyright and intellectual property issues related to faculty-produced material is a broad topic beyond the reach of this paper. The most important requirement is that content in the IR is covered by permissions granted by the copyright owners that are appropriate to the manner in which the content is being used. Such permissions may be granted explicitly through a contract with the faculty member, research group, department, or university.

Permissions may be granted by other means—e.g., commercial publishers that allow self-archiving of previously published materials might just issue a blanket statement on their Web site, and further contract might not be required.

The policies and contracts that govern the IR should be consistent with broader campus intellectual property policy and should reflect the intended use of the content in the repository. If the IR will be used to store materials in perpetuity, such permission should be clearly granted from the copyright holder. The IR should not generally ask for exclusive rights to content. In fact, asking for exclusive rights to content would likely create a discouraging barrier to faculty acceptance.

Policy Issues

Frankly, technology platforms and architectures will not be the most important criteria in the success of your IR. Certainly the IR needs to have certain features and functions, but ultimately the policies that govern your IR and the marketing and outreach done in support of the repository will be most important.

Policies should define the participants and the content that will form your IR. Policies should establish the rights, roles, and responsibilities of individuals and groups that interact with the repository as contributors and patrons/end users.

A challenging question that will likely be faced during the policy development phase will be whether content can be withdrawn from the IR and if so, under what circumstances. This issue will produce considerable debate. If a faculty member leaves the institution can he take the content with him?

Digital file formats and preservation will be another source of discussion. Which file formats will your institution commit to preserving? What format migration strategies will you use? These types of policy questions are critical to settle in the early stages of IR development. They also will may help you determine which software options will be best suited to your needs.

KEY TECHNOLOGIES IN IR SOFTWARE

OAI Compliance

The OAI has developed its Protocol for Metadata Harvesting, or OAI-PMH.

This protocol enables a repository or archive to share metadata using a consistent mechanism. In the bibliographic world, we create Machine Readable Cataloguing (MARC) records that can be shared with other systems (e.g., your consortium, or "WorldCat") to easily spread information about your holdings.

The OAI protocol allows repositories and archives to expose and share metadata (including MARC records and other formats) about the repository content to and with other systems. We already have global services that are harvesting this exposed metadata (OAISter is but one of these; see http://www.oaister.org) that can serve as global catalogs of materials found in IRs and archives.

In one scenario, a faculty member submits a research paper to the repository. The repository supports OAI. After the item is "cataloged" (by the faculty member, a support staff member, or librarian) the item is then available via OAI to OAI harvesting services. These harvesters will run programs that grab the metadata and insert it into their own systems that will serve another, probably larger, audience.

This is preferable to the kind of search capabilities and search accuracy we can find from Google. Google crawls the Web, reads content, and generates a type of metadata, though not particularly structured metadata. Alas, most Web pages do not contain structured metadata of the kind libraries are capable of creating. Thus, Google is left to make assumptions about the contact. OAI-enabled sites, on the other hand, enable structured metadata to be shared that will allow indexing on such fields as title, creator, subject, and date, thus enabling a more precise and productive search.

The technology behind OAI is not important. What matters is that your IR platform is capable of publishing the metadata according to the OAI standard. This will give the content the best chance of wide accessibility worldwide, thus increasing the impact of the author's research. In addition, your institution will increase its exposure, because it will be represented by all of the services that harvest your metadata.

Persistent and Static URLs

Items in your IR should have persistent, preferably permanent URLs. The Web is effective because items can be bookmarked, linked into, and cited. The research papers and other content in your repository should have an address that is durable so that others may find and cite the works. Persistent URLs, or handles, can enable this for long periods.

Various systems can enable this, whether homegrown or external, intermediary services. Many of the IR software platforms enable this off the shelf.

Format Support

You should consider the current and future needs of your IR service in terms of data formats and acquire software that is appropriate to those needs. Consider the types of content you wish to support—research documents, presentations, images, video, for example—and then consider the file types associated with each. These might include PDF, Microsoft Word or Power-Point, JPEG, TIFF, MPEG, and so forth.

Many software platforms are format neutral: they will store bits of any kind. Some types of software platforms may provide enhanced functionality for certain data formats. For example, some programs may automatically translate Word documents to PDF, or TIFF images to JPEG. Some image-specific programs might automatically create thumbnail images.

Workflow

Most software programs provide some support for workflows, which are the movement of documents around an institution for such purposes as sign-off (approval), evaluation, editing, and cataloging. In a repository system the documents do not actually move; rather, various individuals are notified by e-mail that a particular document is ready for their particular task (e.g., reviewing.)

SOFTWARE FOR BUILDING AN IR

DSpace

DSpace, in addition to being the IR service at MIT, is also the name of the open source IR software platform jointly developed by MIT and Hewlett-Packard. It is free to download, and all the source code is available to read or modify. A growing community of universities and other institutions has embraced the DSpace platform. Many institutions are enhancing the software to meet their own needs and are sharing those modifications with others. DSpace provides several key features "out of the box," including OAI-PMH publishing capabilities and persistent URLs to content.

DSpace also offers several workflow options that allow multiple users to collaboratively manage content. For instance, a workflow can be created that allows a faculty member to submit and catalog an item. After cataloging, an automatic notification is sent via e-mail to a librarian (or other user) who is responsible for reviewing the cataloging work. Finally, another e-mail is sent to a project leader who is responsible for final review of the item and catalog record before publishing it to the repository. Workflows are optional. If desired, a single user could perform all the tasks described above.

DSpace supports multiple content formats as well as complex multipart documents, such as a digitized book made of multiple page images.

EPrints

EPrints is another open source software platform for IRs—in fact, it preceded DSpace. It was developed at the Electronics and Computer Science Department of the University of Southampton.

Although it supports a variety of file formats, EPrints was designed for research papers, as the name suggests. There is a large base of installed users of this software, including many outside the United States. Like DSpace, it can be used for theses, gray literature, and the like.

Other Content Management Systems

IR software can be described as a specific type of content management or digital asset management application. Thus, it should be possible to build IRs from any type of content management software. In the commercial world, such software includes Documentum, Vignette, and Artesia. Though not open source, these products typically provide a software developer's kit, or SDK, that will allow customization, extensions, and integrations with other software products. Since they are generic for all types of content management applications, it will probably be necessary to use the SDK for customizations. Depending on the nature of the application you intend to build, commercial software applications may be overkill. Likewise, they may be prohibitively expensive.

ContentDM

ContentDM is a digital library collection management software that is marketed to libraries by OCLC. It is not generally identified as an IR software application, but without a great stretch of the imagination it could be viewed as one. Some organizations are using ContentDM for theses, so a similar project involving faculty research papers could be envisioned. OAI-PMH is supported.

OHIOLINK'S PLANS FOR IRS

What is OhioLINK?

The Ohio Library and Information Network, OhioLINK, is a consortium of Ohio's college and university libraries and the State Library of Ohio. Serving more than 600,000 students, faculty, and staff at 85 institutions, OhioLINK's membership includes 17 public universities, 23 community/technical colleges, 44 private colleges, and the State Library of Ohio. OhioLINK serves faculty, students, staff and other researchers via campus-based electronic library systems, the OhioLINK central site, and Internet resources. OhioLINK is funded by the state of Ohio.

OhioLINK's first service was the shared Central Catalog. This now provides access to a user-initiated, nonmediated online borrowing system containing more than 39.1 million library items. A materials-delivery service is also provided.

OhioLINK continues to expand its service offerings and now maintains a growing digital library infrastructure in support of a variety of resources.

- *Research Databases.* OhioLINK offers more than 100 electronic research databases, including a variety of full-text resources. These databases cover many academic areas at varying levels of detail. Many of the databases are citation indexes. Generally, the user can find out which OhioLINK members possess copies of the cited journal, or they can link to the relevant full-text article. OhioLINK's electronic full-text resources include online dictionaries, literature, and journal articles. Access to the research databases is restricted to valid patrons at OhioLINK member institutions.

- *Electronic Journal Center.* OhioLINK launched the Electronic Journal Center (EJC), a collection of full-text research journals, in 1998. The EJC contains more than 5,700 scholarly journal titles from 70-plus publishers across a wide range of disciplines. More than 3.8 million articles are downloaded each year from the EJC, with a total of more than 10.9 million articles downloaded since its inception.

- *Ebooks.* OhioLINK provides a diverse collection of ebooks, with more than 18,000 titles, some purchased by OhioLINK and others in the public domain and available in the netLibrary collection. The Safari Tech Books Online collection contains 1,800-plus electronic books in computer science, information technology, and related fields. OhioLINK's growing Electronic Reference Book Collection contains 300-plus special-topic reference books, including encyclopedias, handbooks, biographical collections, and guides.

- *Electronic Theses and Dissertations Center.* The Electronic Theses and Dissertations Center (ETD) is a free online database of master's theses and doctoral dissertations from graduate students in participating Ohio colleges and universities.

- *Digital Media Center.* The Digital Media Center (DMC) is designed to archive and provide access to a variety of multimedia material. The DMC contains art and architecture images, audio recordings, satellite images of Ohio, historic Ohio city maps, social studies–related materials, historic archival collections, more than 1,000 educational videos from the distributor Films for the Humanities and Sciences, foreign language videos, and physics demonstration videos. Many collections are accessible worldwide while others are limited to OhioLINK members.

Digital Resource Commons Plans

OhioLINK will extend its DMC infrastructure to support broader content management activities, including IRs. Conceptually, OhioLINK will build something that represents the best features of DSpace with the multi-institution collaborative framework of the EScholarship Repository in the University of California system.

This service will be named the Digital Resource Commons (DRC) and will support the storage, distribution, publication, and long-term preservation of the educational and research materials of participating institutions. OhioLINK members are automatically eligible for this service. The service is being funded by OhioLINK's own budget, with additional money from an Ohio Board of Regents Technology Initiative grant.

Institutions may use the DRC for one or more of the following purposes:

- Faculty research papers such as preprints, postprints or working papers
- Open access self-archiving and publishing
- Student theses and dissertations
- Course materials and learning objects
- Library, archival, and special collections
- Instructional video, audio, and images
- Virtual-reality simulations

A virtually unlimited variety of digital file types and formats will be supported, including text, data sets, image, audio, video, streaming video, multimedia presentations, animations and the like.

Each institution can brand itself in the system and may host a discrete and customized interface to all of its content. To the end user it will appear as an institutional resource as if it were hosted on the servers of an individual campus. There will also be a collective OhioLINK-level branding and ability for searches to retrieve across the institutional collections. This adds a statewide-access dimension of significant value to the individual institutional contributions.

Institutions will have complete control of their own content and how it is accessed. Multitiered security levels will allow content to be shared only to the extent desired. For instance, access to faculty research data may be limited to only a handful of researchers, while a library image collection is published on the Web to the world. Alternatively, content can be restricted to an individual department, to an institution, or to the OhioLINK membership.

Each institution can set its own policies governing the content in its repositories. Likewise, custom workflows can be established to make the most of the personnel involved in each project and expedite the process of content creation and capture.

The service will include robust and flexible cataloging tools to aid in the creation of records that can be searched and browsed effectively by all types of users. Catalog records can be exported in international standard XML formats such as the OAI-PMH.

Through OhioLINK's unique collaboration with the Ohio Supercomputer Center, the content is stored on enterprise-class servers and storage networks. Server computers are stored on the Internet backbone, ensuring maximum availability and speed. A huge storage-area network allows virtually unlimited storage space on our disks. Massive offsite tape and disk backup systems ensure the safety and security of content.

The system, stored at OhioLINK, can be administered locally by library or other designated staff members through standard Web browsers. Programming or system-administration skills and experience are not required. The system is flexible and adaptable and provides IR services without the associated costs of software licensing or personnel to do system administration or software development.

We hope to see a thriving community of institutions contributing to the DRC that will shape the software and services offered over the next few years.

SUMMARY

Many libraries are building IRs for their institutions, using a variety of software platforms. The library is the natural leader of this endeavor on campus because they already serve as stewards of information, digital or otherwise. Software options exist that will allow institutions to build and host these applications locally. Partnerships and consortia may offer alternative options in the form of shared infrastructure for the IR.

RELATED READINGS AND RESOURCES

Bauer, Charly, and Carlin, Jane A. (2003). The case for collaboration: The OhioLINK digital media center. *Journal of Library Administration, 39*(2/3), 69–86.

The California Digital Library opens the eScholarship Repository for working papers. (2002, September). *Computers in Libraries, 22,* 8.

Candee, Catherine H. (2001). The California Digital Library and the eScholarship program. *Journal of Library Administration, 35*(1/2), 37–59.

Crow, Raym. (2002, August). The case for institutional repositories: A SPARC Position Paper. *ARL Bimonthly Report, 223,* 1–4. URL: http://www.arl.org/newsltr/223/instrepo.html. (Accessed July 6, 2005.)

Crow, Raym. *SPARC institutional repository checklist & resource guide.* URL: http://www.arl.org/sparc/IR/IR_Guide.html. (Accessed July 6, 2005.)

DSpace. URL: www.dspace.org.

EPrints Software. URL: http://software.eprints.org.

Harnad, Stevan. (2004, January). "The politics of open access [letter to the editor]." *Information Today, 21,* 16.

Harnad, Stevan. (2001, April 26). The self-archiving initiative. *Nature, 410,* 1024–1025.

Lynch, Clifford A. (2003, April). "Institutional repositories: Essential infrastructure for scholarship in the digital age." *Portal, 3,* 327–336.

Medeiros, Norm. (2003). E-prints, institutional archives, and metadata: Disseminating scholarly literature to the masses. *OCLC Systems & Services, 19*(2), 51–53.

Prosser, David. (2003). Institutional Repositories and Open Access: The Future of Scholarly Communication. *Information Services & Use, 23*(2/3) 167–170.

Queen's Institutional Repository Portal. URL: http://library.queensu.ca/webir/.

Tennant, Roy. (2002, September 15). Institutional Repositories. *Library Journal, 127,* 28, 30.

Tennant, Roy. (2004, February 15). The expanding world of OAI. *Library Journal, 129,* 32.

10

ADAPTIVE TECHNOLOGIES

Jerry Hensley

On the technological landscape today are barriers that in many cases limit or deny a person with special needs access to resources. This chapter will serve as an overview of adaptive/assistive technologies that can be used to eliminate some of these barriers. The adaptations will be categorized based on their core components or general uses.

First, as with any topic relating to this subject matter, is the jargon. The terms *adaptive* or *assistive* are widely viewed as interchangeable. In some schools of thought *assistive* is used when referring to any item that helps perform a task with no permanent effect on the environment in which it is used. For example, a reaching stick or walker would be viewed as being assistive. The term *adaptive* is most commonly affiliated with items that modify the environment in which they are used, even if that modification is very slight. These devices could include things like computer software or power door openers. A more formal definition of these terms could be that provided by the Assistive Technology Act of 1998: "products, devices or equipment, whether acquired commercially, modified or customized, that are used to maintain, increase or improve the functional capabilities of individuals with disabilities."

ISSUES AT HAND

The "playing field" that everyone seeks to level for persons with disabilities is, at present, littered with debris left in the wake of several rapidly evolving high-tech paradigms. None of these items alone, in most situations, is large enough to completely halt a person's progress, but collectively they are making tasks that many able-bodied individuals find simple into acts of great feat and daring.

The area where this debris has piled up the most is along the information superhighway. An emphasis on replacing services that were once performed in person, over the phone, or by mail to with services performed over a Web interface is predominant in nearly all sectors of business. This trend has resulted in compressed timelines, reduced implementation budgets, and strong reliance on emerging or cutting-edge solutions to "Cyberize" the user interaction. This quick-to-market mentality has supplied users with disabilities with many online scenarios that are minimally accessible at best. Even with the emergence of new solutions designed to adapt Web sites and their content, items such as Java applets and completely graphical interfaces remain impenetrable. The increase in the average amount of data users can handle through higher-speed connections has further complicated accessibility by allowing things to become so visual that a user could be interacting with a full-motion video stream in order to perform a particular task or function of a Web site. As we have seen with the piracy issues plaguing the recording and film industries, the laws and federal guidelines governing equal access have been outpaced by the state of the art. In addition, the Internet is truly global, and users are required to visit sites maintained by entities outside the United States, which have no judicial accountability.

The Internet is not the only place where challenges arise. For the past decade there has only been one dominant operating system. Whether you love it or hate it, Microsoft Windows rules the roost when it comes to desktop computers. This overwhelming international adoption of Windows has actually made it easier to provide adaptations to the operating system and to standards-compliant applications running under Windows. When everyone agrees on a standard, or rule, then modifying that standard to meet a variety of unique needs posed by disabilities becomes easier. The local workstation and its applications have become an area of concern because of the emergence of rival operating systems such as LINUX. This operating system is available in many flavors, each of which presents its own challenges when being adapted. Apple Computers Inc., which now uses a more "UNIXish" operating system, has recently launched an initiative to make that product and the programs running within it more accessible. The parade of LINUXs currently being installed have been derived from what is known as open source software, which basically means that each version is different when it comes to the design and support of a particular component of the operating system or an application. While there have been some forays made into adapting LINUX, there is only talk of a standard for doing so, and very few adaptations have emerged that work with all LINUX offerings in a consistently dependable fashion.

ACCESS TECHNOLOGIES

As you, the reader, may or may not be aware, there are a tremendous variety of adaptive technologies to choose from. Most individuals trying to identify adaptive technologies tend to do a quick keyword search in a search engine and read the first four or five offerings from the results page to get an idea of what types of adaptations exist and what audiences they are best suited to. While this method may work in acquiring some knowledge and understanding of what is the "hottest" topic in a particular genre, it will not, in most cases, provide an understanding of what makes the adaptations tick. After completing the quick review, many times a list of the most popular products is compiled and then translated into a purchase order and voilà! While of course this is not true of every situation, it happens more than you might think.

Conveying this somewhat technical and wide-ranging topic of adaptations and their inner workings is a bit challenging but achievable. Instead of focusing on particular products and features, careful consideration has been given to what makes up the technologies and to placing them into broad categories. Once categorized as hardware only, software only, or hardware/software combinations, the purposes of the adaptations will be explained, along with some general guidelines for their implementation.

Hardware Only

Hardware-only adaptations are often referred to as devices. These items are not reliant on a piece of software to make them function. These adaptations are desirable because they can often be used to adapt different environments quickly. The term *assistive* is quite often relevant to this category, since many of these products have no permanent effect on the environment into which they are installed. The technologies at the core of this category are things that in many cases replace an existing piece of hardware but are designed to accommodate specific limitations of the user. While there are few concerns as to compatibility with software and applications being adapted by these items, it is extremely important that the type of connectors, ports, or radio waves being used to establish communications between the adaptations and the workstation be compatible.

Alternative pointing devices allow the user to manipulate the mouse pointer or cursor on a workstation through means other than grasping the mouse and moving it in a particular direction. These means could include movement of the user's head, eyes, cheek muscles, or tongue, which would then be tracked and translated into a signal the mouse driver can understand. Most of these devices are designed to use conventional mouse drivers so they can be quickly implemented and do not require any specialized software. These devices can become as sophisticated as allowing the user to sip or puff in a specific way on a tube placed in their mouth, which is then translated in a box external to the workstations and relayed to the driver, making the mouse move. Many of these pointing systems have become wireless, giving the user more mobility. Since the technical aspect of the pointing device operates in basically the same way as a conventional mouse, the number-one concern when selecting this type of adaptation is the needs of the user(s).

Modified keyboards and key guards are quite prevalent in this category. These keyboards, much like the pointing devices, are intended to mimic the operation of their widely used nonadaptive counterparts. By making the keys larger or smaller and placing them in a variety of positions or recessing them, it is possible to meet a variety of needs. Users who experience spasticity or tremors are challenged with targeting a single key without striking all the keys around it, or depressing the same key several times. A typical feature of adaptive keyboards is one known as sticky keys. This feature allows for a user to execute a multiple key-command sequence by combining the keys as they are pressed singularly and passing them into the computer at once. Keys such as Shift, Alt, and Ctrl can be pressed and then released, and the keyboard will await the next keystroke before sending the completed sequence. For example, to achieve a capital *A* the user would press and release the Shift key and then press and release the *a* key. The device would then send Shift + *a* to the workstation resulting in an *A* being entered.

Key guards or recessed key placements are used to prevent the accidental striking of irrelevant keys. Once the user's finger or other striking instrument, such as a mouth stick, hits the key, it must be raised above the key guard or lip surrounding the recessed key before another key is struck.

Some of these keyboards can become quite sophisticated. These devices allow the development of an overlay or template that is placed on the input device. Special macros or command sequences are attached to the items printed on the overlay. The keyboard may have the intelligence to store these macros in memory, or it may rely on a software component to store and deliver the command sequences to the applications being used. An example of these technologies could be an overlay displaying a picture of a book that, when pressed, would then tell the operating system to open an application that reads books to the user, and possibly open the user's favorite book and begin the reading process.

In the area of visual impairment, the most common device is the CCTV (Closed Circuit Television). The CCTV began as a black-and-white video camera connected to the back of a television set and then mounted on a pole over the top of a tray that would hold the printed material. Many of these early models required the person using them to change the focus of the camera as often as once or twice per line of text, depending on the amount of rise in the page from the edge to the binding. Current versions of these devices have come a long way. Most models available today are full color and have automatic focus as well as a variety of features that allow the user to tailor the image displayed on the screen to accommodate their particular pathology. A large number of these units can also be patched into a computer system so that the content being read on the CCTV will display along with the output of the computer. This feature is particularly useful when transcribing information into the computer. Technology has progressed so far in this area that there are even several models of highly mobile CCTVs on the market, some being roughly the size of a portable DVD player.

The devices that appear in this category are too numerous to list, but some other items that belong here are things like switches (often used in place of mouse buttons), joysticks, device/monitor mounting arms, and copy stands. In fact, the slate and stylus (a tool for manually embossing Braille onto paper), Braille typewriter–like embossers, and Braille printers would be included. Braille printers do typically need a driver to be installed on the workstation, but like the pointing devices and keyboards, the driver is a very common one and is most likely available on any workstations the printer might be hooked to.

Software Only

Today's adaptive technology marketplace is bursting at the seams with new and innovative software solutions. An entire book could be devoted just to the most common of these offerings and rewritten every six months just to keep up. Many of these products can be grouped together based on the disability population they are designed to assist.

Sensory-motor adaptations comprise a fair percentage of these programs. These programs are mainly designed to improve input speed and accuracy. Several of the programs can draw something known as a virtual keyboard on the screen, and when a user clicks the mouse or holds the mouse pointer still, or dwells, on a specific key, that key will be sent to the computer as input. Settings that allow the user to customize the dwell time, key size, and visual layout of the keyboard are common. Some of these applications also combine themselves with other products to offer something known as word prediction. Word-prediction software can be obtained in a stand-alone package or found as an added component of other applications. Word prediction is a process in which a list of words is displayed somewhere on the screen, and as the user types characters the most likely words in that language are displayed in their order of likelihood. For example if a user were to type "wh," the list would display (1) *what*, (2) *where*, (3) *why*, (4) *when*, and so on. The user could simply click on the word in the list they wish to use or say/type the number, depending on the application. Newer word-prediction solutions are "artificially" intelligent and keep track of every word the user has ever selected so that when a recommendation list is displayed it is most probable that the first word is the correct word for that user based on history and context.

Cognitive/expressive augmentation adaptations are those in which the solution accommodates the loss of brain function or ability to express things. These packages will often allow the user to interact with the computer on a level that suits them. For example, a small toolbar may be visible on the screen with pictures of the most common activities on each tool. The user can then click the tool they recognize as appropriate for the task they want to complete, and the computer will perform one or multiple steps to complete the task. For example, a picture of a snowflake might be used to activate a series of commands that will adjust the thermostat in the house to 68 degrees.

Mild to moderate vision impairment can be accommodated by a software solution. In most cases this solution comes in the form of a screen-enlargement program or screen magnification software. These applications typically interface directly with the display drivers in the computer that control the video card. On newer workstations this process is accomplished without changing the video driver and instead linking the screen-enlargement software to the video driver. The intention of these types of software is to adjust the visual display of information in as many ways as possible to meet the needs of several pathologies. You would most likely find the ability to magnify text, change colors, select different views, and track particular objects. The flexibility of these packages can vary considerably. One package may magnify text by up to four times the normal size while another can go to sixteen times the normal size. Certain packages can even change the color of particular screen elements such as mouse pointers, cursors, title bars, and menu highlights. The complexity of the packages typically relates to how many different visual disabilities can be accommodated. Many times an application such as this is used in conjunction with a larger-size monitor, but this is not required to make the program operate.

While there is a plethora of other areas in which software adaptations are making a mark, these are some of the more prominent ones. Software adaptations may also be found for captioning video for the deaf, teaching sign language, or translating documents into Braille.

Hardware/Software Combinations

The category *hardware/software* combinations consists of items that have been represented by all of the previously mentioned classifications, as well as by the marriage of hardware and software, which has traditionally been done to achieve an adaptation for the most involved of disabilities. Bringing these two powerful forces together poses some challenges, but as standards emerge in the mainstream technology industry the challenges are sometimes reduced.

Input alternatives like pointing devices and keyboards can be partnered with software that will allow them to do things like monitor a user's electrical activity in different areas of their brain to direct the movement of the mouse, or to scroll through a list of character choices until the correct one appears, and select it. This is done by combining a program that the user trains to their brain-wave activity with a headset that uses tiny electrodes to pick up the signals. A user can think calm, soothing thoughts to move the mouse up or ponder analytically to move the mouse down. A keyboarding solution from this category could involve the projection of a keyboard hologram onto a flat surface, which is monitored by software to determine which area of the hologram the user places an object in or looks at to ascertain what key is pressed and then pass it on to the application.

The idea of pairing keyboards and software can also be seen in the evolution of a number of portable devices used for purposes ranging from taking notes in Braille to completely replacing an individual's ability to speak. Special design considerations are used to manufacture this equipment for a specific purpose. Blind users might require that the device they are using to take notes be able to talk to them and also offer the output in the form of mechanical dots that raise and lower to create Braille. Users in need of augmentative speech may be best served by a note taker that also allows them to program a series of common phrases and assign the phrases to an icon so they can press the icon and have the phrase spoken. Capabilities of these augmentative speech devices and note takers has expanded to include complete environmental control, access, cellular phone integration, and in many cases an impressive set of productivity applications for word processing, calendar management, or spreadsheet creation.

The most rapidly growing population, from the viewpoint of technology usage, are individuals with learning disabilities. Features that appear widely in software for this group are things like verbalized output, real-time dictionaries, highlighting, and use of a scanner for inputting material. In many cases the user finds it nearly impossible to comprehend printed information. When the computer reads the content, the comprehension rate is dramatically increased. While this is primarily a software adaptation, it is heavily reliant on speech synthesizers, sound cards, and document scanners. These applications can range in sophistication from the ability to verbalize highlighted text from a word processor to being able to import an HTML document from the Web or scanned materials and redisplay them in a way the user determines as best for them.

Blindness-related adaptations have historically laid the foundation for this category. These applications rely entirely on a speech synthesizer, refreshable Braille display, or sound card. In recent years the use of the sound card found in the workstation has become prevalent for creating speech output. The use of a text-to-speech application, or screen reader, is a complicated process. Users who are completely blind or severely visually impaired have no access to the mouse and therefore must perform every task by using a series of keyboard commands. It is commonplace for a reasonably proficient blind user to have roughly fifty key commands readily in mind to control basic functions of the operating system and core applications. An additional 50 to 100 commands may need to be learned for use in controlling the speech output and directing the screen reader in what the user needs to hear. Top those off with another 50 or so commands that are unique to a particular suite of applications the user needs to perform desired tasks and you have in some cases nearly 200 commands racing around the user's mind. Other than the fact that a blind user is not going to use the mouse, it is important to understand how applications like this function.

The application resides in the computer's memory and uses some hooks and other helper services to monitor what is being displayed on the screen. The application then breaks this information down into its component parts to construct something known as the Off Screen Model (OSM). The OSM is a database of all the elements that make up the screen (even some that are not visible to the sighted user) and their specific attributes. For example, when exiting an application in which work is open and unsaved, the application will display a box asking the user if they wish to save or to abandon exiting and return to the application from which they came. This box could comprise several elements. These elements might include a Title bar, Minimize button, Maximize button, Close button, dialog box text like "Do you wish to save?" Yes button, No button, Cancel button. The user can then navigate through each of these elements by using assigned keystrokes such as the Tab key to move forward one element and Shift+Tab to move back an element. Once the element is marked, the space bar can be pressed to activate it. These products are making tremendous progress in access to the content displayed in Web browsers. But if the code used to generate a particular Web page or pages is not written in an accessible fashion, the adaptation cannot make it become accessible. It is extremely important to ensure that HTML content be developed in such a way that it complies with all standards and guidelines for accessibility, thus maximizing the screen reader's usefulness.

The previously mentioned screen-enlargement programs can also spread into this arena by adding the capability to supply speech output to users who are transitioning from large print toward total text-to-speech functions. This makes the adaptation dependent on hardware to generate the speech and causes it to function very much like a text-to-speech application when this mode of output is being used.

Computers talking to users has occurred for quite some time. Users talking to computers is a younger technology but is rapidly evolving. This solution is frequently referred to as speech recognition. Speech recognition is performed by using software designed to listen to a user's speech and compare it to a dictionary of prerecorded speech patterns to attempt to determine what the user is saying. These adaptations ship with a generic dictionary file that is most compatible with enunciated midwestern English. This dictionary, or speech profile, requires the user to train or customize it to their specific speech patterns. This training can take from 2 to 10 hours initially and in most cases is a continual process during the course of using the program. These applications place very intense demands on system resources and usually require a robust workstation to function satisfactorily. These programs are also very dependent on a clear signal that is not interfered with by background noise or static resulting from poor-quality microphones or connections. It is crucial to observe the environment where this technology will be used and also carefully investigate various microphones and their appropriate installation and use. These packages offer a range of functionality, from simply allowing the user to speak text into a proprietary word processor, to providing voice command and control of the operating system and multiple applications, and being able to speak text into practically any program.

Hardware blended with software is indeed powerful. This power comes with some unique challenges but is in many cases the only alternative. Ensuring compatibility in these installations is important to successful integration.

PUTTING IT TOGETHER

Many times a user has needs that have either not been identified or that the user does not acknowledge. It is recommended in all cases when a user is obtaining and using adaptive technologies that he or she consult with a trained professional specializing in the relevant technologies that will best accommodate them. These professionals can be found in several different ways. The way that works best is to interact with individuals in the community who use these services. Locating and contacting organizations comprising persons who have a specific disability can yield an incredible amount of information. Many times just asking around among your close friends will turn up someone who knows of a person with the type of disability being addressed. If these methods do not prove successful or are not convenient, you might try contacting social service organizations in your area. The method of last resort, which tends to work well, is to contact your public school district and speak to the special education or special services coordinator. School systems are required by law to provide adaptations and to include students with particular disabilities in the classroom. Many districts will be aware of at least a minimal number of resources or can direct you to someone who can help.

Once a professional assessment has been performed and adaptations selected, the user will in most cases need some training. Usually the person performing the assessment can direct the user on how much training is typical and where that training is available. When selecting an adaptation, it may be wise to investigate the amount of specialized training needed for its use and if there are resources available from the vendor to help in this process.

Obviously, the software, hardware, or both will need to be installed and configured. Some applications are quick and easy in this respect, but others require extensive knowledge, tools, or time. Making it through this phase of acquisition and implementation is sometimes difficult, but it is worth the effort. A good installation can make the success of an adaptation much more likely.

PAYING THE PRICE

As with any project, there has to be a price tag. Budgeting for an adaptive workstation is very similar to buying any piece(s) of technology. Getting input during the assessment process can often clear up questions about formulating the budget. It is also advisable to look at technologies that can be purchased in component parts over time if possible.

Funding of such adaptive equipment is sometimes quite a challenge. Again, community resources can be a great benefit. Contacting state and federal agencies for help in locating any grants or special one-time funding vehicles to help get technology established is highly recommended.

The budget should of course include funding for any needed training or additional materials to facilitate training. Many times the budget is developed to implement, but not to maintain, the adaptations. In some markets the life cycle of a single version of an adaptation can be as short as six months. Planning for upgrades or investing in a maintenance agreement to keep the technology current is a wise choice. Upgrades can, in some cases, cost nearly as much as the original purchase.

The final step in this process is to investigate special pricing or promotions. You can sometimes obtain information on these options from the vendor or from the person doing the assessment. In the adaptive technology marketplace there are several developers who sell products through regional representatives. Finding out who is representing the developer for the geographic area you are purchasing in may also yield some information on pricing or promotions.

A plan and careful attention to detail will bring to pass an implementation resulting in ongoing use, and increased productivity for the individual requiring the adaptations. The ties established throughout this process with agencies and personnel that are experienced in disability issues should be maintained to increase understanding and a support network. In many cases the relationships gained through this process can assist and benefit the user as much as the technology itself.

11

LET'S GET DIGITAL

Samantha K. Hastings and Elise C. Lewis

This chapter introduces you to some of the technology behind digital image management. We begin with a discussion centering on preservation and access issues. Digitization of analog materials is not preservation, and it is important to understand why and what you want to digitize before you begin any project.

Next, we explore digital image-capture options and some of the technology currently used, from scanners and cameras to the computer equipment needed. Then, we take you through some of the terminology and concepts you need to know for purposes of quality control, regarding such issues as file formats, compression, and image resolution.

Finally, we conclude with a brief introduction to metadata and content indexing for digital resources. Standards are the key to these efforts, and we provide a list of resources for more information about standards development in this field.

PRESERVATION

Digitization can help preserve precious materials: making high-quality digital images available electronically can reduce wear and tear on fragile items. This does not mean, however, that digital copies should be seen as a replacement for the original piece. Digital files, too, are not permanent and must be maintained. In particular, they periodically need to be transferred to new formats when one format becomes outdated. Even after digitization, original documents and artifacts must still be cared for. Thus, preservation remains a secondary benefit of digital projects. If preserving a collection is deemed a higher priority than increasing access to it, purchasing acid-free folders, encapsulating fragile documents, or otherwise improving storage conditions would be a better use of resources. But, there are benefits to making collections or items available digitally:

- Can be viewed from anywhere, at any time
- Viewers can find what they are looking for quickly and independently
- Can save staff reference time by making frequently requested materials available on the Web
- Can enhance images electronically so that they can be viewed with greater legibility
- Increased use of collections facilitates learning and scholarship

DIGITAL LONGEVITY, PRESERVATION, AND MIGRATION

Preservation of digital objects does not guarantee that a digital version of any material will survive over time. Formats and technology change. The National Archives recommends that public records and permanent copies of documents be preserved in an eye-readable format. Eye-readable refers, for the most part, to paper copies or microforms that can be viewed on readers or with the naked eye.

Born Digital

The Library of Congress has presented a report defining the issues in the preservation of objects that are born digital. Perpetual care of digital objects is more challenging than perpetual care of paper. Preservation programs for objects born digital are urgent and require immediate attention (Library of Congress, 1999).

Some Thoughts on Preservation

- Digitization is *not* preservation. If the goal is to preserve existing collections, then use of traditional preservation through acid-free photocopies or preservation-quality microfilm will prove to be more cost effective.
- For truly unique, damaged, and fragile materials, establish a process to conserve and rehouse the originals, then make digital versions accessible.
- Consider if the materials have sufficient value to users to justify digitization and preservation. Can digitization achieve the goals of the organization? Is the cost appropriate and can the staff resources be devoted to the project? If the answer to any of these questions is no, then the digitization project is not viable.
- Long-term preservation of the digital collection will require an investment in infrastructure and digital content management. Does the organization have the

resources to create the infrastructure and management strategy? Where will the funding come from to create such an infrastructure?

- Scanning from the originals is always best, unless they are too fragile or damaged to survive handling. An alternative is to scan from high quality microfilm, if available.

- At this time, there is no single, off-the-shelf solution for either hardware or software appropriate for the preservation and digitization needs of libraries and museums. OCLC is working on solutions with CONTENTdm, a software package for digital collections management (OCLC, 2004).

- *Fragile storage media.* Digital materials are especially vulnerable to loss and destruction because they are stored on fragile magnetic and optical media that deteriorate rapidly and can fail suddenly from exposure to heat, humidity, airborne contaminants, faulty reading and writing devices, human error, and even sabotage.

- *Technological obsolescence.* Digital materials become unreadable and inaccessible if the playback devices necessary to retrieve information from the media become obsolete or if the software that translates digital information from machine- to human-readable form is no longer available.

- *Legal questions surrounding copying and access.* Libraries, archives, and other cultural institutions have limited and uncertain rights to copy digital information for preservation or backup purposes, to reformat information so that it remains accessible by current technology, and to provide public access.

As key activities aimed at ensuring the long-term accessibility of our digital heritage, digital archiving (the process of identifying, collecting, and making material accessible in its current format) and digital preservation (managing this material to ensure it remains accessible as technology changes) have gone hand in hand. While much early attention was directed toward the archiving side, digital preservation has increasingly been a focus of activities. A common definition for digital preservation or digital archiving can be found in the UK's CEDARS project: "Storage, maintenance, and access to a digital object over the long term, usually as a consequence of applying one or more preservation strategies, whereby a digital object in this sense, is any resource that can be stored or manipulated by a computer and can be applied to digitized and born-digital material" (CEDARS, 2002).

When organizations put up unique collections in digital formats, they are responsible for obtaining rights to publish and permissions to use or distribute material. Just because a library or museum has documents in the collection does not mean it owns the digital reproduction rights. Rights and permissions will be one of the important criteria to consider when selecting collections to digitize. Determining the legal status of selected collections or documents is an important step in the selection process. It is important to document any efforts to seek permissions to use material, keeping track of all steps taken to look for unidentified copyright owners or to ask for a right to digitize the materials, and publish them online. A routine established for

---

RESOURCES

- Cornell University-Copyright Term and Public Domain

  http://www.copyright.cornell.edu/training/Hirtle_Public_Domain.htm

- For a more detailed discussion of copyright restrictions, take the Copyright Crash Course from the

  University of Texas.

  http://www.utsystem.edu/ogc/intellectualproperty/cprtindx.htm

- Digital Millennium Copyright Act (DMCA). Find out more about this on the Library of Congress

  copyright site.

  http://www.copyright.gov/

Figure 11.1 Resources on Copyright

documentation must be in place as part of the selection process to keep you and the organization safe from copyright infringement. Figure 11.1 lists Web sites with information on copyright.

IMAGE CAPTURE OPTIONS AND TECHNOLOGY

Converting Analog to Digital

During image capture, an image is "read" or scanned at a defined resolution and dynamic range (digitizing). Scanning is a process that generally resembles photography or photocopying. Depending on the type of capture device, the image to be scanned may be placed either in front of a digital camera lens (on a stand or tripod) or on a scanner. A shot is taken, but instead of exposing the grains on a piece of negative film or on a photocopying drum, light reflects off (or through) the image onto a set of light-sensitive diodes. Each diode responds like a grain of film, reading the level of light it is exposed to, except that it converts this reading into a digital value, which it passes on to digital storage. The number of distinct readings, taken vertically and horizontally, determines the resolution of the scanned image. The possible number of values that are represented by each pixel is the dynamic range of the image.

Desktop scanners, or flatbed scanners, resemble photocopying machines. Source material is placed flat on the glass and captured by diode arrays that pass below it. Desktop scanners do a good job of capturing images for which you lack the slide or neg. Flatbed scanners require source material to be no larger than the glass and to lie face-down and flat, which excludes a lot of archival materials.

Slide scanners resemble small boxes, with a slot in the side big enough to insert a 35 mm slide. Slide scanners can generally scan only 35 mm transparent-source materials.

Digital cameras are used in place of a normal film camera. The resolution of digital cameras is fixed and expressed as a pixel ratio. Professional digital cameras go as high as 2036x3060. Source material is placed on the stand and the camera is cranked up or down in order to fit the material within its field of view. This allows the scanning of different sizes of originals.

Drum scanners resemble mimeograph stencil machines from the 1960s; source material is placed on a drum, which is then rotated past a high-intensity light source that captures the image. Drum scanners tend to offer the highest image quality, but they require flexible source material of limited size that can be wrapped around the drum.

Outsourcing, or contracting out, image processing is an alternative to doing it in house. The cost-effectiveness of each approach depends on the volume and type of materials being scanned, and the economics of this equation change rapidly with market conditions. Whether scanning is done in house or off site, scanning quality can vary widely. Off-site sources offering image capture vary considerably in the levels of quality they provide. A variety of sample images should be sent to several vendors and quality compared before any project is actually begun.

THE TERMINOLOGY OF DIGITAL CAMERAS

The charge-coupled device (CCD), which is made up of millions of tiny points called pixels, sees what a frame of film in a traditional camera sees through the lens with the shutter open. The light collected by the CCD is then converted into data, and this data is then stored on the camera's memory card. The image can then be viewed on the camera's display screen, downloaded onto a computer, edited, stored, and also printed in photographic quality. A simple example of a CCD is shown in Figure 11.2.

There is no need to buy additional memory to take more photos, because you can reuse the same memory over and over again, just as you do with the memory in your computer. You can also view the image you have just taken. If you are not happy with it, you can delete it, leaving space for another one. Once an image is downloaded from the camera to the computer, it is then possible to use image-editing software, included with most digital cameras, to adjust brightness, contrast, and color levels, sharpen images, and even apply special effects. The images can be sent to friends via e-mail or uploaded to Web sites for public viewing and access.

Pixel Array

The camera capture levels are rated by pixel array in megapixels. Since *mega* means "million," one megapixel equals one million pixels. In general, a two- megapixel digital image will yield a good 5″× 7″ print when printed on photo-quality paper on a good inkjet printer, and a tolerable 8″×10″ print. A three-megapixel image can produce an 8″×10″ print that is hard to distinguish from a print of the same size made from a 35 mm film image.

A two- or three-megapixel image file can take a long time to download to your computer. In addition, if you are going to use your digital photo on a Web site, the resolution of your computer monitor will not be able to show all the detail you have captured. For this reason, most good digital cameras give you a choice so that you can record images using only a portion of the maximum available pixels and thus create a smaller file.

Storage Devices

Exactly how many images can you store on a 128 MB card? It depends on the exact size of the file created by a given camera, as well as the resolution that you select. On cameras that give you a choice of different resolutions to record your photos, the number of images you can capture will vary as you switch back and forth between resolutions. To give you a rough idea, a three-megapixel model with a 128 MB card can fit more than 125 images at the lowest resolution.

Light Sensitivity

One of the great benefits of traditional film cameras is the wide choice of different types of film and different film speeds. One of the drawbacks of most digital cameras is that the light sensitivity of the chip that captures the image is relatively slow, the equivalent of ISO 100 film. That means you'll find it hard to take pictures in low light without using a flash.

Digital Camera Power

Digital cameras cannot work without power. There is no such thing as a manual digital camera. You will need to put batteries in your camera or plug it into an electrical outlet via an adapter.

The Viewfinder

Many digital cameras have an optical viewfinder similar to a viewfinder found in a compact 35 mm camera. With almost all digital cameras it is also possible to preview the image using the camera's liquid crystal display (LCD) screen, meaning it's possible to hold the camera away from your face while capturing images and viewing them on the screen.

From Camera to Computer

To transfer the images from the digital camera's memory card to your computer, the camera is normally connected to the computer via a cable either the Serial Port or the Universal Serial Bus (USB) port. The only exception is if the camera uses a smart card or CD-ROM to store the images, in which case you can just put the disk into the computer's appropriate drive and transfer the image in the same way that any other files would be transferred—using the copy-and-paste, drag-and-drop, or Save As functions.

Modern computers have a USB port, which is much faster at transferring images than a serial port. Not all operating systems support the operation of the USB port, but in many cases connecting the camera to a computer with a USB port is as simple as plugging in the cable. Setting up the serial port is slightly more complicated and requires the installation of software (supplied with the camera).

Many digital cameras now being produced have USB support only and no serial-port support. To use these cameras you must have an operational USB port. In some cases, where a USB port is not available on the computer and the camera offers no serial-port support, it is possible to purchase an optional card reader, which can be connected to the computer's parallel port (printer port). The card reader is then used to read the card rather than the camera's internal card reader/writer. Many digital cameras also have an A/V output, which allows you to view your images on a TV screen in a slide-show style.

COMPUTERS AND DIGITAL IMAGES

Once the images have been transferred from the camera into the computer (downloaded) you may want to edit them in some way, perhaps to change the size of the image, the contrast and brightness, the color balance, or any of the many other options available using image-editing software. The speed and memory capacity of the computer is much more important for the editing processes than for the process of downloading the images.

Although it is possible to edit an image with an older computer, the process is likely to be slow and possibly restrictive. If you only plan to edit one or two images here and there, then an older computer will probably do most of the things you would want, although it will probably be slow. If you will be editing large numbers of images at a time (more than 10) then the speed and memory capacity of an older machine is likely to make your experience slow and unproductive.

What Factors Do I Need to Look for in a Computer?

Many factors affect the overall usability of a computer for digital editing. The CPU (Central Processing Unit) is the brain of the computer. CPUs have been getting faster and more powerful since their beginnings.

Processing Speed

Speed is normally measured in megahertz (MHz), or millions of cycles per second. The first Pentium computers had CPUs that ran at speeds of 90–200 MHz. That means the CPU was processing 90 million to 200 million cycles of instructions each second. Today, CPUs available to consumers work at speeds of over 4 GHz or 4,000 MHz. Obviously, this makes the processor much more powerful, and other factors such as the number of instructions the CPU can compute during each individual cycle have also improved, increasing performance along with the increase in raw speed (MHz).

A fast CPU will make life easier for your digital-photography studio. Adding effects to images and changing color and contrast levels requires the computer to execute a large number of processes. A fast processor can help make the editing experience a smoother, more productive one.

Screen Size and Resolution

The size of a computer screen is another important factor to consider when setting up a computer system for digital image editing. For example a digital image that comes from a 3-megapixel camera will have a resolution of 2048 $\times$ 1536 pixels, while most 17-inch computer monitors have a resolution of either 800 $\times$ 600 pixels or 1024 $\times$ 768 pixels. Add to this all of the option boxes image-editing software displays on the screen and it is easy to see why a large screen is beneficial. A 19-inch or 20-inch monitor makes image editing much easier.

Graphics Card

The graphics card plugs into the computer and, in turn, the computer monitor plugs into the graphics card. Many graphics cards are advertised with 3-D acceleration features. The features of the 3-D graphics cards are not used when processing digital images and will make no difference to the performance of the system.

What is important with graphics cards is to be able to support a high enough resolution in full-color mode for the monitor. The maximum resolution that a graphics card can produce is related to the amount of RAM the graphics card has. The graphics card has its own RAM, separate from the computer's RAM. The more RAM the card has, the higher the resolution it can produce in full-color mode. Most new graphics cards can easily support a 17- or 19-inch monitor in full-color mode. A graphics card with 8 megabytes of memory will support a 17-inch to 19-inch monitor in full color

SCANNING TERMINOLOGY

Pixel

A digital image is a picture composed of a set of pixels (picture elements), similar to dots on a newspaper photograph or grains on a photographic print or the dots in a pointillist painting. The number and nature of the pixels in your image determines how well it reflects the object it represents. *Resolution* and *bit-depth* are another way to say *number* and *nature*.

A pixel is the smallest piece of information a digital image is made from. The image cannot be broken down to smaller points. Your computer monitor uses pixels. A 15-inch monitor with a standard screen resolution of 800 × 600 has 480,000 pixels, and a 17-inch monitor at 1024 × 768 has 786,432 pixels.

Because modern digital cameras can record images in resolutions up to 2048 × 1532, which is over 3 million pixels (3 megapixels), the image will be much larger than most computer monitors, resulting in the need to scroll the image across the screen.

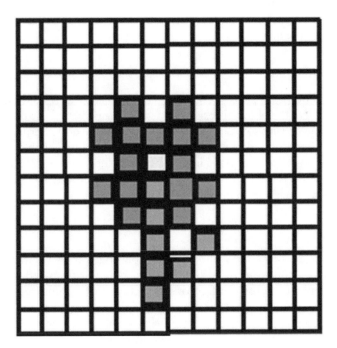

Figure 11.2 Here is very simple example of a camera's CCD, it has a resolution of 12 × 12 = 144 pixels. Each dot that makes up the flower is 1 Pixel. Because the resolution is so low the image has very limited detail.

Figure 11.3 An Enlarged Image

The right-hand image in Figure 11.3 has been enlarged to 800 times the original size (digital zoom). Now you can start to see the individual pixels that make up the image.

Resolution

The digital-capture process creates a digital object that should be considered a picture of the object. It exists as a whole image that can be displayed by manipulating viewing software such as Photoshop or Adobe Acrobat. Digital objects can be displayed in various measures of resolution, such as pixels, as in pixels per inch (ppi), dots, as in dots per inch (dpi) or lines, as in lines per inch (lpi), which is used for halftones. Achieving a basic understanding of the technical issues relating to image quality is important.

Scanning

Let's look at the process of scanning a photograph. A scanner passes a horizontal bar consisting of a light source and a discrete series of light-sensitive elements across the face of the picture to be converted to digital format. The scanner records the amount of light at each point for each individual light-sensitive element. This process is called sampling. As the scan head is passed over the picture, it periodically samples, or records, how much light is reflected from the surface of the item being scanned.

The scan head moves across the length of the picture, building up the image one line at a time. Each scan line contains a series of picture elements, which are the recorded color and lightness values. The image data actually contains only lightness values, but three passes are made by the scan head to obtain the three lightness values that define the color of each picture element. Thus, each pixel has color and lightness properties associated with it. The values of these properties depend on what color model (the number system used to represent a given color) is used. Each pass records the brightness values for each of the primary colors (red, green, and blue) used in what is called the additive color process. In this method, the lightness and color values are combined; the lightness of any pixel is the sum of the individual color values.

Bit Depth

Every pixel in a screen display has a certain number of colors available to it, depending on the capabilities of the video display card within the computer system and the number of colors available within the assigned color space. Most video display cards available can display millions of colors, although many older systems will support only up to 8-bit displays, or 256 colors. Graphic designers who want to display an image on the Internet will work to reduce the number of colors available in their image in order to decrease its file size. An image with a smaller file size will load faster on a Web page.

Bit depth or color depth refers to the maximum number of colors available for pixels in a display, expressed in bits (2-bit, 8-bit, 16-bit, 24-bit, 32-bit, etc.) A 2-bit displayed pixel can only show a maximum of 4 colors, an 8-bit pixel can show 256 colors, and a 24-bit pixel can show 1.6 million colors. The rule is: the greater the bit depth, the larger the image size. Reducing bit depth, however, decreases image quality.

In general, a designer looks to decrease file size while maintaining maximum image quality. This can be done by reducing bit depth to an optimal level and reducing the height and width dimensions of an image through cropping or resizing. When scanned, an image is broken into a grid of blocks. The lightness or darkness and color of each block is described by the computer using 1's or 0's. These are called bits. Depending on the scanning mode used, the blocks will be black or white (Bitmap mode), a range of grays from black to white (Grayscale mode), or colored (RGB mode—red, green, blue—or CMYK mode—cyan, magenta, yellow, black). A comparison of these modes is shown in Figure 11.4.

Bitmap images contain 1 bit of information per pixel (1 = black, 0 = white). Grayscale images contain 8 bits of information per pixel. There are 256 possible levels of gray for each pixel in a grayscale image, and each level can be described by a combination of a string of eight 1's and 0's (2 to the 8th power = 256). A color image made up of a combination of red, green, and blue (RGB) contains 24 bits of information for each pixel (8 bits of informa-

Modes (Bit Depth)

Bitmap:	1 bit/pixel (i.e.: 0 or 1) Black and White
Grayscale:	8 bits/pixel (i.e.: 01010101) 256 Shades of Grey from Black to White
RGB:	8 bits/channel (Red, Green, Blue) Millions of Colors.
CMYK:	8 bits/channel (Cyan, Magenta, Yellow, Black) For printing only.

Figure 11.4 Modes (Bit Depth)

tion for each color, or 3 colors × 8 bits = 24 bits). 8 bits of information can also be referred to as 1 byte.

Sometimes as you modify, print, scan, or save an image you have an option to choose the color mode. Figure 11.5 provides a basic definition of each mode.

Graphic Images and File Sizes

File size is an important consideration when working with graphics. Generally, there is a direct relationship between the file size and the quality of the image—the better the quality, the larger the file size. In addition, the larger the file size, the more time needed to display the graphic. The file size of a graphic is a function of the image size in pixels and the color depth and can be calculated using the following formula: **(image size in pixels × color depth in bits) / 8.** Note that the file sizes are generally expressed in bytes. Because color depth is in bits and there are 8 bits to a byte, dividing by 8 changes the calculation from bits to bytes (see Figure 11.6).

Color Modes

Black and White	Provides access to only two crayons or colors: black and white.
Grayscale	Provides access to 256 shades of gray ranging from black to white.
16 Color	Provides access to only 16 colors, but if you do not like a color you can swap it for 16 million other color variations at any time.
256 Color	Provides you with 16 times as many colors, and you can also swap or change from 16 million color variations at any time.
32 Bit Color	Primarily used for CMYK images used for printing full-color artwork. Makes an image more complicated without any real benefit for normal use.

Figure 11.5 Color Modes

Bit Conversion

1 Bit = 0 or 1	1 Kilobyte (Kb) = 1024 Bytes	1 Gigabyte (Gb) = 1024 Mb
1 Byte = 8 Bits	1 Megabyte (Mb) = 1024 Kb	1024 gigabytes = 1 terabyte (Tb)

Figure 11.6 Bit Conversion

The Figures 11.7 and 11.8 show the file size and quality for various image sizes and color-depth combinations.

File Formats

File types, or formats, refer to the different formats in which image files can be saved. How you intend to use a file will determine the format you should use. Listed are the most common types of digital files.

File Size and Quality of Various Image Size and Color Combinations for a 640x480 Screen Resolution.

Image size (pixels)	Amount of screen used	Color depth (bits)	Number of possible colors	File size (bytes, approximate)
320x240	Quarter screen	8	256	77,000
320x480	Half screen	8	256	154,000
320x480	Half screen	16	64,000	307,000
320x240	Quarter screen	24	16 million	230,000

Figure 11.7 640×480 Screen Resolution

File Size and Quality of Various Image Size and Color Combinations for a 1024x768 Screen Resolution

Image size (pixels)	Amount of screen used	Color depth (bits)	Number of possible colors	File size (bytes, approximate)
512x384	Quarter screen	8	256	197,000
512x384	Quarter screen	16	64,000	393,000
512x384	Quarter screen	24	16 million	590,000

Figure 11.8 1024×768 Screen Resolution

- Photoshop (.psd): This file type is the native Photoshop format. This is the optimum file to use while you are working in Photoshop, because it enables layers and all of the layer functions.
- Bitmap (.bmp): This is a Windows-compatible file format. It is lossless, meaning that no file information is discarded when you save the file.
- EPS (.eps): This is an Encapsulated Postscript file, a great option for line art and for when you want to import line art into page-layout programs.

- GIF (.gif): The Graphics Interchange Format is an excellent choice for the Web. Use the File+Export Gif89a to create transparent GIFs.
- JPG (.jpg): This is the Joint Photographic Group Experts file format. This is a lossy format: depending on how you save the file, image information for the sake of conserving file size is discarded. You can adjust these settings as you save. This is a great option for the Web.
- PDF (.pdf): This stands for Portable Document Format. It works in conjunction with Adobe's Acrobat product, which is another option for Web publishing.
- PICT (.pct): This is a Macintosh-only file. It contains a Macintosh resource fork.
- Pixar (.pxr): This is for use with high-end graphics machines and 3-D imaging programs.
- PNG (.png): This format is an alternative to the GIF file format. It is great for Web publishing and is growing in popularity. It enables you to save your files and allows them to download progressively over the World Wide Web.
- Raw (.raw): This format saves files as a stream of bytes. This is good for moving between applications and computer platforms, but it is better if you can decide on an actual format that will serve all of your cross-platform needs, such as JPEG or TIFF.
- TIFF (.tif): A very common format, the Tagged-Image File Format works cross-platform and uses lossless LZW compression (meaning that no image data is discarded from an image as it is compressed). This is a common file format for archival copies of an object.

Choosing the right format to store your images is an important decision that will affect their future accessibility. There is no one format right for all purposes. You will have to decide what your goals for scanning and storing images are. If your images are for the Web, you will want a format that makes for speedy downloads by creating files with a small footprint and creates the most compact image possible using compression techniques. On the other hand, if your purpose is to create a digital archive, then you will want a format that retains the highest fidelity to the original image and does not sacrifice any quality in order to save space.

Interpolation, or "How Come it's Fuzzy When I Blow it Up?"

Interpolation is the term used to describe what happens when a portion of a digital image (or the entire image) is enlarged. When enlarged (meaning increasing the image size through the Image Size dialogue, or using the transform tool to increase the size of an object), the computer must interpolate, or make up, color or grayscale values for the new pixels. To do this, the computer reads the values of adjacent pixels in the original image, then uses those values to estimate the values for the new pixels created between the original pixels.

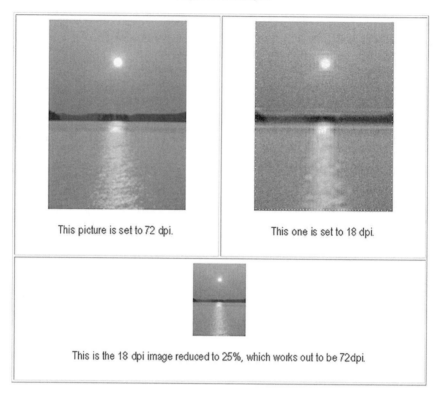

Figure 11.9 Interpolation Examples

Because interpolation is an estimation, an image or object with a high level of detail or crispness will suffer some amount of softening or blurriness, depending on the amount of enlargement. When an image or object is reduced, Photoshop tosses out excess pixels. The image sharpness remains because no interpolation of pixels has occurred (see Figure 11.9).

Compression

There are two approaches to storing pictures once they have been converted to digital form. The first approach is to save the image data sent by the scanner to the computer mostly unchanged from its original form. This is called a non-lossy or lossless image file format because it literally saves the original data from the scanned image. This is the kind of compression you would want for store storing archival copies of your images. For example, if the scanner found that a particular spot on your picture had a lightness value of 255, that same lightness value will be retained when the picture is saved. A small snapshot may need tens of thousands of small dots to give an acceptable image quality. Each dot of color requires three values, one for each primary color used to simulate real colors in the printing or display process. This means even a small color snapshot will require large amounts of space to record all those numbers.

This leads us to the second approach, which attempts to solve the problem of images consuming large amounts of storage. In most images there is redundant data that can be left out when storing the image and recreated when the image is displayed or edited. There may be large areas of an image that are exactly the same color. Instead of recording long strings of the same lightness values, the software records one lightness value and how many times it appears. The original image data is either lost or so changed it cannot be completely reconstructed when you want to use the image again. Saving space this way is called compression. This kind of compression is called lossy compression because it loses some of the original image quality.

There is a limit to the amount of storage space that can be saved by compressing an image this way. More effective ways were created to save images in even more compact forms. The JPEG method, for example, uses knowledge about human visual perception to discard image data it deems unimportant. This data is not redundant data like we saw before, but actually significant data from the original picture. The idea is that we will not miss the data we cannot see. Just enough image data is eliminated so that we still perceive an image with the same quality as the original. People, however, have different abilities to perceive image quality, so an image saved with a certain amount of compression may appear of high quality to one person and of moderate quality to another. Once saved, there is no way to retrieve the original quality image without scanning the original picture again.

The method used to compress the picture may create artifacts in the image. Artifacts are features introduced to the image by the mathematical rules used in compression. These occur when the elements used by compression to make up the image become large enough to see, and subtle banding or color shifts from the original occur. Often, the lossy format acts like a one-way street: you can scan and save an image with acceptable quality, but you cannot open the image again to edit it without losing some quality.

Color Management

Color management is perhaps the most complex and problematic issue of digital imaging and scanning. A WYSIWYG (What You See Is What You Get—pronounced *wizzy-wig*) Color Management System allows you to accurately simulate on the monitor screen what you can expect to see in real life. Traditionally, color management was done prior to going to the printing press. The work was done by printers or by bureaus servicing the print industry. The emphasis was exclusively on printing with ink on paper. Consequently, the conversion from RGB to CMYK was done on the fly right in the scanner. All of the retouching, image manipulation, special effects, and color correcting were done on the CMYK file.

METADATA: INDEXING IMAGES

The field of metadata has exploded into a major area of investigation and development over the past several years. As information becomes more of a commodity, its management is of interest to a broad spectrum of organizations. This stands in rather strong contrast to the situation in the pre-Internet era, when the standardized management of information was more or less restricted to libraries. This broadening of the metadata environment includes many new players and applications and requires the library to think in new ways if it is to reassert its leadership in this area.

Indexing content description will be an important activity in the management of any digital-image project. The indexed terms add to the ability to search and retrieve digital images and other objects from a database. Metadata is described as information about information. It is a very complex and tricky aspect of your digital project. Good metadata is required for successful retrieval and management of digital assets, so you will want to explore several options. Like so many areas of a digital project, there has not been an accepted standard adopted by all information centers.

There are several types of metadata that can be recorded for different purposes. Most information centers use basic types of metadata, but other elements may be added to meet additional information needs. Oftentimes, the types of metadata may overlap. Here are some examples of types or classes of metadata:

- *Administrative metadata.* Information about rights, authorship, and ownership
- *Structural metadata.* Used by viewing software
- *Content metadata.* Description, title, etc.
- *Technical metadata.* Primarily used in house to indicate types of files, dates created, software use, etc.
- *Descriptive metadata.* Similar to content metadata; usually a controlled vocabulary describing the subject of the image

Why do we need metadata? It is useful for resource identification, resource discovery, authentication, rights management, provenance, version control, resource-system use, and tracking of users. It will become even more important as we continue to develop digital-library systems that are interoperable.

Here are some examples of metadata elements (the list is not in any way comprehensive):

- *Terms and conditions.* Metadata that describe the rules for use of an object. Terms and conditions might include an access list of who may view the object, a conditions-of-use statement might be displayed before access to the object is allowed, a schedule (tariff) of prices and fees for use of the object, or a definition of the permitted uses of an object (viewing, printing, copying, etc.).

- *Administrative data.* Metadata that relate to the management of an object in a particular server or repository. Some examples of information stored in administrative data are the date of last modification, the date of creation, and the administrator's identity.

- *Content rating.* A description of attributes of an object within a multidimensional, scaled rating scheme assigned by some rating authority; an example might be the suitability of the content for various audiences, similar to the well-known movie-rating system used by the Motion Picture Association of America. Note that content ratings have applications far beyond simple filtering of levels of sex and violence. Content ratings are likely to play important roles in future collaborative filtering systems, for example.

- *Provenance.* Data defining the source or origin of some content object; for example, of some physical artifact from which the content was scanned. The data might also include a summary of all algorithmic transformations that have been applied to the object (filtering, reductions in image density, etc.) since its creation. Arguably, provenance information might also include evidence of authenticity and integrity through the use of digital signature schemes; or, authenticity and integrity information might be considered a separate class of metadata.

- *Linkage or relationship data.* Data indicating the complex relationships between content objects and other objects. Some examples are the relationship of a set of journal articles to the containing journal, the relationship of a translation to the work in its original language, the relationship of a subsequent edition to the original work, or the relationships among the components of a multimedia work (information on synchronization between images and a soundtrack, for example).

- *Structural data.* Data defining the logical components of complex or compound objects and how to access those components. A simple example is a table of contents for a textual document. More complex examples include the definition of the different source files, subroutines, data definitions in a software suite, SGML- or XML-tagged books, or other complex works.

Metadata Standards

You will need to select a metadata standard and format to guide the creation of your indexing. Two commonly used indexing standards are Visual Resource Association and the Dublin Core metadata schema. It will be useful to create a set of protocols and guidelines for the project staff who will be indexing. Consistency is important to achieve valid data.

Founding Initiative: Dublin Core Metadata Initiative

The Dublin Core Metadata Initiative (DCMI), begun in 1994, hoped to create a simplified metadata convention that would provide more effective resource discovery on the Web. Over the past five years, it has developed and refined a set of 15 elements—the Dublin Core Element Set (DCES)—for resource description to facilitate discovery. The DCMI has broad international participation from librarians, digital-library specialists, the museum community, and other information specialists. Advocates claim that the DCES has distinct advantages over traditional cataloging methods in terms of simplicity, interoperability, and extensibility.

DCMI, which is hosted by OCLC, represents a concerted effort by OCLC to extend the leadership role it has played with physical resources into the world of digital resources. The DCES plays an important role in one of OCLC's latest projects, the Cooperative Online Resource Cataloging (CORC) project, which is examining the use of new Web-based tools and techniques for cataloging electronic resources. One important aspect of CORC is that it examines the mechanics and economics of different levels of representation, whereby resources can be described simply using the DCES and, when appropriate and economically feasible, described more completely using traditional cataloging techniques (Machine Readable Cataloguing, or MARC).

The rapid changes in technology have increased the importance of technical metadata. It is important to include the software version, file types, and date of creation to ensure the longevity of the resources. Many research organizations spend a great deal of resources to develop the best standards of practice. These Web sites provide information on different metadata schemas:

- Berkeley—Making of America 2 (http://sunsite.berkeley.edu/moa2/)
- Getty Institute—Metadata Comparison (http://www.getty.edu/research/institute/standards/intrometadata/index.html)
- Library of Congress—Core Metadata Elements (http://www.loc.gov/standards/metadata.html)
- National Information Standards Organization (http://www.niso.org/committees/committee_au.html)
- Research Library Group—Preservation Metadata Implementation Strategies (PREMIS) (http://www.rlg.org/en/page.php?Page_ID = 7821)
- VRA's Introduction to Metadata (http://www.vraweb.org/metadata.html)

SUMMARY

We hope this information has been helpful and, if nothing else, you now know what to ask and where to start looking for answers. It is important that you realize that this information, like all technical specifications, changes constantly. Keep using guidelines such as the *NINCH Guide to Good Practice* (see the referenced list at the end of this chapter) for updates, and subscribe to mailing lists that discuss these issues. Imagelib (imagelib@listserv.arizona. edu), Museum Computer Network, OCLC and the Visual Resource Association all have active lists. Also, please do not hesitate to contact us with specific questions by sending an e-mail to elewis@unt.edu or hastings@unt.edu.

REFERENCES

Cedars Preservation Strategy. (2002). *Cedars Guide to: Digital Preservation Strategies.* URL: http://www.leeds.ac.uk/cedars/guideto/dpstrategies/dpstrategies. html. (Accessed August 10, 2004.)

Library of Congress. (1999). Conservation Implications of Digitization Projects. National Digital Library Program and the Conservation Division. URL: http://lcweb2.loc.gov/ammem/techdocs/conservation.html.   (Accessed August 10, 2004.)

National Initiative for a Networked Cultural Heritage (NINCH). (2003). *The NINCH Guide to Good Practice in the Digital Representation and Management of Cultural Heritage Materials.* URL: http://www.nyu.edu/its/humanities/ /ninchguide/. (Accessed August 12, 2004.)

OCLC. *Content DM.* Digital Collection and Preservation. URL: http://www.oclc. org/contentdm/about/default.htm. (Accessed August 12, 2004.)

SELECTED BIBLIOGRAPHY

Kathleen M. Webb

The following bibliography lists articles, books, and Internet sites that provide information about the technology topics covered in this book. Given the speed with which some of these technologies change, only the most current resources are listed. Web documents were included if they were published on the Web site of an association or a corporate site that has a professional or financial interest in the topic. This standard was used to provide some hope of the document still existing a year or two from now. These resources may offer an introduction to the topic, definitions, or methods of applying these technologies in libraries.

The bibliography is divided into four sections: digital initiatives (digitizing technologies, Rich Site Summary (RSS) and blogs, and XML and metadata); networking (network security and wired and wireless networking); building and connecting online information repositories (institutional repositories, open archives initiative [OAI], and OpenURL); and service technologies (adaptive technologies and Radio Frequency Identification [RFID]).

DIGITAL INITIATIVES

Digitizing Technologies

Chapman, Stephen, & Comstock, William. (2000, December 15). Digital imaging production services at the Harvard College Library. *RLG DigiNews*. URL: http://www.rlg.org/preserv/diginews/diginews4–6.html#feature1.

This summary of the planning, setup, and implementation of the Harvard College Library's digital production service provides an excellent introduction to the resources necessary for digitization projects. The section on equipment will be especially useful to beginners.

Cornell University Library Research Department. (2003). *Moving theory into practice: Digital imaging tutorial.* URL: http://www.library.cornell.edu/preservation/tutorial/contents.html.

This tutorial funded by the National Endowment for the Humanities takes the user through the process of converting materials into digital form and making them accessible. Chapter six provides details on the technology necessary for image creation, file management, and image delivery.

Hughes, Lorna. (2004). *Digitizing collections: Strategic issues for the information manager.* London: Facet.

While this book provides advice for beginning and managing a digitization project, it is the last three chapters that explain the technologies needed to make the change to digital format. There is an excellent section on the processes and technologies for the digitization of rare and fragile materials. The chapter on audio and moving images provides several suggestions for digitizing various formats. Numerous resources are listed throughout each chapter.

Lee, Stuart. (2001). *Digital imaging: A practical handbook.* New York: Neal-Schumann.

Anyone beginning a digitization project will find this book useful. It explains an easy-to-follow process for a digital project. Chapter three provides explanations of digital imagining techniques and equipment.

RSS and Blogs

Cohen, Steven. (2004, February). RSS. *Computers in Libraries,* 28.

This one-page primer defines the standard, lists the groups working on it, explains the pros and cons, and provides a brief list of additional resources.

Gahran, Amy. (2004, May 4). What are Webfeeds (RSS) and why should you care? *Contentious Weblog.* URL: http://blog.contentious.com/archives/000180.html.

This 12-part tutorial is an excellent starting point for anyone interested in using or publishing a Web feed. It provides an introduction to Web feeds, including how they work and subscribing to and publishing your own feed. Key terminology and concepts are hyperlinked to other parts of the tutorial and to additional tutorials created by the author. There are also links to resources outside this Web site.

Lowery, Shelley. (2004, June 29). Syndicate your headlines using RSS. *Marketing Aces.* URL: http://marketingaces.com/articles/syndicating.html.

The author of this article provides an example of XML code necessary to write a document for an RSS reader. There is a link to an RSS validator and a script to translate the RSS file to display on a Web site.

XML and Metadata

Baca, Murtha. (2000). *Introduction to metadata: Pathways to digital information.* URL: http://www.getty.edu/research/conducting_research/standards/intrometadata/index.html.

The first version of this work was published in print in 1998. This updated, online version provides a beginner with a thorough introduction to metadata. The author explains its importance and describes the necessity for crosswalks, which are mechanisms for converting metadata from one schema into another.

Caplan, Priscilla. (2003). *Metadata fundamentals for all librarians.* Chicago: American Library Association.

The first section of this book explains principles applicable to all metadata schemes. Subsequent sections introduce the reader to general descriptive metadata schemes such as Dublin Core, as well as descriptive schemas for disciplines such as architecture and education. The book ends with chapters on administrative, structural, and rights metadata.

Coyle, Karen. (2004, February). MODS. *Computers in Libraries,* 21. "A Dozen Primers on Standards." (2004, February). *Computers in Libraries,* 18.

The theme of this issue is "Making Standards Understandable." There are several excellent primers dealing with digital initiatives. Each primer defines the standard, lists the groups working on it, explains the pros and cons, and provides a brief list of additional resources.

Gilmour, Ron. (2003). *XML: A Guide for Librarians.* Chicago: LITA.

Written for librarians, this book provides a great introduction to XML and related technologies. There is an overview of the basics of XML and explanations of XML's relevance to libraries.

Kennedy, Shirl. (2004, February). RDF. *Computers in Libraries,* 27.

McDonough, Jerome. (2004, February). METS. *Computers in Libraries,* 20.

National Information Standards Organization. (2004). *Understanding metadata.* Washington, DC: NISO. URL: http://www.niso.org/standards/resources/ UnderstandingMetadata.pdf.

This free publication from the National Standards Organization is a excellent resource for metadata novices. It begins with a definition of *metadata* and a description of what it does. There are examples of metadata records as well as a case study explaining how a historian would use metadata. The glossary and bibliography are excellent.

Tennant, Roy (Ed.). (2002). *XML in libraries.* New York: Neal-Schumann.

This is an excellent introduction to creative uses of XML in libraries. This book describes how libraries are using XML to improve interlibrary loan services, enhance catalog records, and publish materials online.

Wagner, Richard, & Mansfield, Richard. (2003). *XML All-in-One Desk Reference for Dummies.* New York: Wiley.

The audience for this book is XML novices. There are seven quick reference guides in this one volume. It begins with an introduction to describing data with XML and walks the user through defining structures and then presenting the XML in print or via a browser. Later chapters look at emerging technologies and advanced applications for working with XML.

NETWORKING

Network Security

Ayre, Lori. (Ed.) Connie Lawthers and Jeff Eisenberg. (2003). *Library and computer network Security.* URL: http://www.infopeople.org/howto/security/.

The Infopeople Project is an IMLS-supported project dedicated to providing technology-related training to the staffs of California libraries. This site on network security provides a comprehensive explanation of security issues from risk assessment to writing a security policy. It contains sections on security for users, workstations, servers, and networks. Technical terms are hyperlinked to definitions, and the annotated Webliography provides additional resources.

Banerjee, Kyle. (2003, May). How much security does your library need? *Computers in Libraries,* 12.

This article provides an excellent starting point for library staff because it explains why hackers might target libraries and how library systems may become compromised. The author follows these sections with brief explanations of tools that can help, including firewalls, antivirus software, and network-analysis tools. The article ends with suggestions for protecting library systems and actions to take if a system has been hacked into.

Cain, Mark. (2003). Cybertheft, network security and the library without walls. *The Journal of Academic Librarianship, 29*(4), 245–248.

Open proxy servers are a security risk, and this article explains why. Given the prevalence of open proxy servers on university campuses, this should be a topic discussed in academic libraries. This article will help librarians learn about the issue so that they can work with their campus computing units to help address the problem.

Cobb, Cheryl. (2003). *Network security for dummies.* New York: Wiley.

This book assumes a basic knowledge of networking yet is still a valuable reference tool for the librarian new to the security aspect of networking. Each chapter can stand alone; however, some topics mentioned in later chapters were defined and explained in the beginning of the book. Topics include assessing network risks, establishing security policies, security mechanisms such as firewalls and software, and access control.

Kanabar, Dina, & Kanabar, Vijay. (2003, May). A quick guide to basic network security terms. *Computers in Libraries,* 24.

When a simple definition is needed, this article is perfect. The authors have selected four terms for common computer attacks (*denial-of-service, spoofing, spyware,* and *viruses*) and four terms for protecting systems (*digital certificates, digital signatures, firewall,* and *SSL*). Each concept is defined, with an explanation of how it works.

Klingenstein, Nate. (2004, February). Shibboleth. *Computers in Libraries,* 30.

This is another one-page primer that defines the standard, lists the groups working on it, explains the pros and cons, and provides a brief list of additional resources.

Wired Networking, Including Local Area Networks (LANs) and the Internet

Leiden, Candace, & Wilensky, Marshall. (2003). *TCP/IP for Dummies* (5th ed.). New York: Wiley.

The authors of this book assume that the reader is a networking novice, so it begins with a good introduction to networking. Readers who are familiar with networking basics might begin with the section on protocols and addresses and then move on to the section on configuring TCP/IP services. The CD-ROM that accompanies the book contains tools and utilities for managing and using an intranet or the Internet.

Lowe, Doug. (2004). *Networking for Dummies* (7th ed.). Indianapolis: Wiley.

This book provides a basic introduction to LANs. Part one is an introduction to the topic, part two describes how to build a network, part three introduces readers to the job of network management, and part four explains how to connect a local network to the Internet.

Molyneux, Robert E. (2003). *The Internet under the hood*. Westport, CT.: Libraries Unlimited.

Specifically written for information professionals, this book provides a comprehensive look at networking, from LANs and wide area networks to the Internet. The language is accessible for a beginner. Each chapter ends with an excellent list of resources, and there is a useful glossary at the end of the book.

Wireless Networking

Drew, Wilfred (Bill), Jr. (2003). Wireless networks: New meaning to ubiquitous computing. *Journal of Academic Librarianship, 29*(2), 102–106.

The author, owner of the Wireless Librarian Web site, touts the virtues of wireless networking for libraries and other academic units. This article contains an explanation of standards, a brief discussion of planning for wireless, examples of uses in academic libraries, and a list of resources.

Engst, Adam, & Fleishman, Glenn. (2003). *The Wireless Networking Starter Kit*. Berkeley, CA: Peachpit Press.

This book begins with an introduction to networking basics, which can be skipped if you have a basic understanding of networking or have read some of the other networking resources listed in this bibliography. Chapter three provides a good explanation of how wireless networks work and includes a description of the necessary hardware. Later chapters explain how to build and provide security for a wireless network.

McGeehon, Carol. (2003, March). Could the flexibility of wireless solve a problem for you? *Computers in Libraries*, 15.

The problems described in this article are ones faced in all libraries. These three examples of a wireless implementation will show how any library could benefit from a wireless network.

BUILDING AND CONNECTING
ONLINE INFORMATION REPOSITORIES

Institutional Repositories (IR)

Horwood, Lynne, Sullivan, Shirley, Young, Eve, & Garner, Jane. (2004). OAI compliant institutional repositories and the role of library staff. *Library Management, 25*(4/5), 170–176.

In this article the authors are encouraging libraries to work collaboratively with their campus IT staff and teaching faculty to create e-print repositories. The article describes issues that may surface, including intellectual-property rights, peer review, preservation, and metadata creation.

Lynch, Clifford. (2003, February). Institutional repositories: essential infrastructure for scholarship in the digital age. *ARL Bimonthly Report 226*. URL: http://www.arl.org/newsltr/226/ir.html.

In this ARL report the author defines and explains the strategic importance of an IR. He argues that IRs should be looked at as an essential infrastructure service that supports the scholarly and research goals of an academic institution. Librarians who are still unsure of the importance of IRs will find this article thought provoking.

Smith, MacKenzie, Bass, Mick, McClellen, Greg, Tansley, Robert, Barton, Mary, Branschofsky, Margret, Stuve, Dave, & Harford Walker, Julie. (2003, January). DSpace: An Open Source Dynamic Digital Repository. *D-Lib Magazine*. URL: http://www.dlib.org/dlib/january03/smith/01smith.html.

DSpace is probably the most well known platform for building an IR. This article explains the functionality and design of the DSpace system. The graphics that accompany the description of the information model and the technical architecture will appeal to visual learners. The second part of the article describes the implementation of DSpace at MIT and will be useful to libraries considering a similar project.

Peters, Thomas. (2002). Digital repositories: individual, discipline-based, institutional, consortial, or national? *The Journal of Academic Librarianship, 28*(6), 414–417.

Examples of, and arguments for and against, consortial digital repositories are presented in this article. While the author concludes that consortia may play a role in the repository movement, there are important reasons why shared repositories could cause problems. Any institution weighing the cost and benefits of building their own IR or working with a consortium will find this article useful.

Open Archives Initiative (OAI)

Caplan, Priscilla. (2004, February). OAI-PMH. *Computers in Libraries*, 24.

This primer defines the Open Archives Initiative Protocol for Metadata Harvesting (OAI-PMH), lists the groups working on it, explains the pros and cons, and provides a brief list of additional resources.

Hagedorn, Kat. (2003). OAIster: A 'no dead ends' OAI service provider. *Library Hi Tech, 21*(2), 170–181.

OAIster is perhaps one of the best-known sites using OAI-PMH to collect and present scholarly digital resources. This article describes how OAIster was developed and tested, as well as the issues that surround metadata harvesting and presentation. This article will help librarians understand how the service works, and, perhaps more importantly, it will provide some ideas to keep in mind when creating a digital repository that may be harvested.

Needleman, Mark. (2002). The open archives initiative. *Serials Review, 28*(2), 156–158.

This article presents a brief explanation about how OAI-PMH works and lists several interesting projects being developed by libraries and library-related groups. The description of these projects helps explain the importance of OAI to libraries.

Open Archives Forum. (2003, 14 October). *OAI for beginners—The open archives forum online tutorial.* URL: http://www.oaforum.org/tutorial/.

This tutorial from the Open Archives Forum describes the OAI-PMH. The overview, history, and glossary sections are especially appropriate for beginners looking for a good introduction to the topic.

OpenURL

Beit-Arie, Oren, Blake, Miriam, Caplan, Priscilla, Flecker, Dale, Ingoldsby, Tim, Lannom, Laurence W., Mischo, William H., Pentz, Edward, Rogers, Sally, & Van de Sompel, Herbert. (2001, September). Linking to the Appropriate Copy: Report of a DOI-Based Prototype. *D-Lib Magazine.* URL: http://www.dlib.org/dlib/september01/caplan/09caplan.html.

Linking to journal articles via OpenURL resolvers would be relatively simple if every person in the world could link to the same copy of a journal article. Given the proliferation of journal aggregators, however, the necessity for finding the "appropriate copy" for each user is clear. This article describes Digital Object Identifiers (DOIs), CrossRef, the appropriate copy problem, and a project offering a possible solution.

Dahl, Mark. (2004, February). OpenURL. *Computers in Libraries,* 26. A Dozen Primers on Standards. (2004, February). *Computers in Libraries,* 18.

There are two primers dealing with OpenURL and linking technology. Each one defines the standard, lists the groups working on it, explains the pros and cons, and provides a brief list of additional resources.

Grogg, Jill, & Fergeson, Christine. (2004, February). Oh, the places linking will go! A state of the union report. *Searcher,* 48.

Beginning with a brief explanation of the language of linking, this article describes the evolution of linking technologies and services. It contains a brief explanation of the limitations of OpenURL version 0.1 and how version 1.0 is addressing those problems. Homegrown linking projects are summarized, and commercial linking products are examined for new features. The article ends with a look at the future of linking services.

Hellman, Eric. (2003, July). OpenURL: Making the link to libraries. *Learned Publishing*, 177.

Although this article could be seen as an advertisement for a linking-service vendor, it offers a unique explanation of why linking services are so important. The author uses a personal story about a failed attempt to find an article while he was a graduate student at Stanford University. The story and the subsequent explanation of how a linking service could have provided him with enough information to find the article will appeal to faculty. Librarians should consider using this article when explaining linking services to their campus communities.

Kennedy, Shirl. (2004, February). "DOI." *Computers in Libraries*, 19.

Langston, Marc, & Tyler, James. (2004). Linking to journal articles in an online teaching environment: The persistent link, DOI, and OpenURL. *The Internet and Higher Education*, 7, 51–58.

This article describes using persistent URLs from within databases, DOIs, and OpenURL to create online reading lists for classes. The authors are teaching faculty who are promoting the use of linking services when creating online instruction modules.

Sidman, David. (2003, June). *What is a Digital Object Identifier (DOI)?* URL: http://www.contentdirections.com/materials/WhatistheDOI_files/frame.htm.

While intended as a marketing tool, this PowerPoint presentation from Content Directions is also an excellent description of a DOI and how it works with an OpenURL.

SERVICE TECHNOLOGIES

Adaptive Technologies

Bryant, Diane Pedrotty, & Bryant, Brian. (2003). *Assistive technology for people with disabilities*. Boston: Allyn and Bacon.

Each chapter of this textbook begins with an outline of the chapter, a list of learning objectives, and a "Making Connections" paragraph that provides the reader with a list of questions to keep in mind while reading the chapter. This book is written for the person who needs an introduction to assistive technology with an emphasis on devices and services. The illustrations and photographs are especially useful.

Lazzaro, Joseph. (2001). *Adaptive technologies for learning and work environments* (2nd ed.). Chicago: American Library Association.

This is an excellent introduction to the types of technologies available to assist people with special needs. It contains chapters detailing technologies for persons who have vision impairments, who have motor, learning, and speech disabilities, and who are deaf or hard of hearing. The chapter on funding adaptive technology will be useful to most libraries that are looking to add these services. The several appendixes list products and resources for persons with disabilities. There is also a brief explanation of disability-rights laws.

Mates, Barbara. (2000). *Adaptive technology for the internet: Making electronic resources accessible to all*. Chicago: American Library Association. URL: http://www.ala.org/editions/samplers/mates/.

As Head of the Library for the Blind and Physically Handicapped in Cleveland, Ohio, this author is an expert in using assistive technologies to provide library services. This book focuses on the technologies necessary to provide Internet access to people who have vision impairments. It contains chapters on funding these technologies as well as on training library staff to use them; appendixes that list vendors and organizations that make these technologies available; a glossary; and a list of further readings. This book is also available in print.

Mates, Barbara. (2004, May/June). Computer technologies to aid special audiences. *Library Technology Reports*, 6–96.

This issue includes several useful chapters, including "Library Website Design and Database Access" and "Information Access for People with Disabilities." It contains information about the latest assistive hardware and software, as well as
information on funding these technologies. Each product description includes a URL for the manufacturer's site.

Radio Frequency Identification (RFID)

Boss, Richard W. (2004, May). RFID technology for libraries. *TechNotes*, 19. URL: http://www.ala.org/ala/pla/plapubs/technotes/rfidtechnology.htm.

This is an excellent introduction to the uses of RFID technologies in libraries. The author examines the benefits to staff and operations, describes the disadvantages of the technologies, and explains some early problems encountered with RFID technology (also having contacted users of the systems to document that they have been solved). The end of the article describes how the systems work and includes approximate costs.

Boss, Richard W. (2003, November/December). The technology of RFID. *Library Technology Reports*, 18.

This entire issue is dedicated to the topic of RFID. This particular chapter explains the technology in detail. There is a comprehensive description of the different types of tags and readers as well as places where readers can be used. Other chapters include an extensive glossary, interviews with users of RFID systems, and sample RFP requirements.

Wadham, Rachel. (2003, September/October). "Radio frequency identification." *Library Mosaics*, 22.

This brief article provides a simple definition of RFID and describes current uses in libraries.

GLOSSARY

Frances Rice

802.11x a set of specifications for wireless local area network (WLAN) communications. Currently, there are four specifications, 802.11, 802.11a, 802.11b, and 802.11g. All specifications are based on Ethernet protocol, are used for short distance transmissions, and, depending on which specification, have transmission rates up to 54 megabits per second. Developing standards include 802.11e (Quality of Service), 802.11f (Access Point Interoperability), 802.11h (Interface) and 802.11i (Security).

Access Point equipment or software that connects wireless clients to a wired LAN, in a similar manner that hubs connect wired clients. Each access point can serve multiple users.

AP see Access Point

API see Application Programming Interface

Application Programming Interface a set of rules, or instructions, developed to allow two operating systems or application programs to communicate and share information.

Assistive technology a device to help individuals with special needs live more independently and be self-reliant. Assistive technologies include computer workstations equipped with specialized software and/or adaptive devices.

AT see Assistive technology

Attribute used to describe properties of a database such as a field or table. It can also describe a display element in HTML tagging such as color or text size.

Backbone the main transmission line connecting smaller multiple data lines of a local area network. In a wide area network or the Internet, the backbone is used to describe the set of paths local or regional networks use for long-distance interconnections.

Blog a personal journal that has been posted on a Web site. Typically, blogs reflect the personality of the author and contain philosophical reflections, commentaries, and links to their favorite sites. Authors of blogs are referred to as bloggers, and blogging refers to updating a blog.

Bridge a device that reads data packets sent in one local area network to determine if the destination node, or address, resides within the same local area network or if the packet needs to be forwarded to another interconnected local area network. Bridges record which nodes reside on which network, allowing subsequent messages to be forwarded to the right local area network. Bridges reduce the amount of unnecessary network traffic by directing packets toward a specific destination instead of broadcasting them to multiple destinations.

Broadband a high-speed, multiple-band network dividing the wider bandwidth of coaxial cable or fiber optics into various independent transmission channels, providing the ability to transmit data, voice, and video simultaneously.

Broadcast to send the same message to all users on a network. Broadcast has also been used to describe the process of searching multiple resource databases simultaneously.

Browser a graphical interface program used to search, view, listen, and interact with information available on the World Wide Web. The most popular browsers are Microsoft's Internet Explorer and Netscape Navigator.

Cascading Style Sheet a World Wide Web Consortium specification addressing layout and style elements of a Web page that are referenced by subsequent Web pages throughout a single Web site. Modifications to display elements such as fonts, colors, and sizes are easily achieved by editing the CSS.

CMS see Content Management System; see Course Management System

Collision a crash of data transmissions from two separate devices that share the same data channel, as in an Ethernet network. Waiting a random amount of time and resending the transmissions restores the garbled data transmission.

Content Management System software used to manage content on a Web site. The key feature of a CMS is that it provides content managers with the ability to create, edit, and delete content from a Web site without the expertise of a Webmaster. Documentum and Interwoven's TeamSite are commercial examples of content-management systems.

Cookie information sent by a Web server and downloaded on a user's computer. The small amount of information is reused by a Web server to help identify a user throughout the session. Some cookies are left on user computers to maintain user-defined preferences associated with a specific Web site. An example of cookie information is the online shopping cart feature, which stores information about a user and prepopulates the order form with this information.

Course Management System a software program that integrates numerous course functions—such as rosters, grade books, online quizzes, Internet e-mail, syllabi, and more—and makes them available over the Internet. Two of the most popular software vendors for course-management systems are WebCT and BlackBoard.

Crosswalk a translation table describing relationships and equivalents between data elements of two or more metadata platforms. Search engines use crosswalks, also referred to as metadata mapping, to search effectively across heterogeneous databases.

CSS see Cascading Style Sheet

Dark fiber fiber optic cables transmit pulses of light, instead of the frequency signals used in coaxial cables. The term *dark fiber* refers to fiber optic cable that is not in use. Alternately, the term *lit* is used to describe an active cable.

Digital Object Identifier a permanent identifier assigned to a Web file or Internet resource. The digital object identifier is submitted to a centrally managed directory and is used in place of the URL for the Web file. When Web file addresses change, the central directory is updated and redirects any requests for the Web file to its new address.

Document Type Definition elements included in an XML document defined and stored within a document type definition file, which is sent along with XML documents. This ensures that documents will display or print as intended.

DOI see Digital Object Identifier

DTD see Document Type Definition

Dublin Core a fifteen-element metadata schema used to describe a wide range of electronic resources, and used to access Web resources. The data element set has been identified by an international, cross-disciplinary group of professionals from various fields of scholarship.

EAD see Encoded Archival Description

Encoded Archival Description a predefined set of XML markup tags developed exclusively for the creation of electronic archival finding aids. An encoded archival description is an example of a document type definition.

Encryption the process of encoding data packets into a secret code as they are transmitted over a network or Internet, preventing anyone except the receiver from reading the data packets.

Ethernet describes local area networks using coaxial cable carrying radio frequency signals between networked devices with data transmission rates of 10 megabits per second, referred to as 10BASE-T. Fast Ethernet, or 100BASE-T, provides for transmission speeds up to 100 megabits per second, and gigabit Ethernet transmits data at 1,000 megabits per second.

Expect a UNIX or Windows scripting language which automates keystrokes, eliminating the need for a physical response to command prompts of an interactive program such as backups, transferring files via FTP, or downloading software updates.

eXtensible Markup Language very flexible programming language used to tag or mark up documents and data for the Web. Unlike HTML, XML does not have a predefined set of tags, but rather, designers can create their own tags to indicate specific information. HTML concerns itself with display features of Web pages, not with the interpretation of information contained in the text. XML files are used to mark up the text into data, which can be interpreted between applications and between organizations. XML can be used independently of HTML or in conjunction with HTML.

eXtensible Stylesheet Language used in conjunction with XML to describe the formatting and display of data transmitted over the Web. Because XML does not provide predefined formatting tags, an XSL is written to define the display or print version of one XML document and can be reused in subsequent XML documents.

FDDI see Fiber Distributed Data Interface

Federated Searching the ability to search over multiple information systems with a single search. Federated searching does not perform indexing of Web databases; rather, it translates search requests into a syntax understood by the various Web databases chosen to be searched. WebFeat and Sagebrush are commercial examples of federated searching.

Fiber Distributed Data Interface a transmission standard used by networks built on fiber optic cable. It provides for transmission rates at 100,000,000 bits per second, ten times faster than Ethernet.

File Transfer Protocol a widespread technique used to move files between remote servers. This is commonly used on Internet sites to allow anonymous users to download files.

Firewall a combination of hardware and software that acts as a buffer between internal networks and the Internet. Network traffic, or data packets, is screened against a table of rules. Disallowed packets are not permitted into the network. Firewalls protect an internal network from intruders or hackers.

Frame relay an interface used in wide area networks to determine how packets of data are routed. Network traffic is routed from information received through a frame relay, insuring greater throughput in the network.

Frames a term referring to an HTML programming technique that loads multiple Web pages at the same time from one master HTML file. Frames create the look of stand-alone sections within one Web page, enabling some sections to remain visible while other sections change.

FTP see File Transfer Protocol

Gateway an access point between two dissimilar systems, such as a company's local area network and the Internet. Using hardware or software setup, a gateway translates between two different protocols.

Gigabit Point-of-Presence an access point for high-speed Internet connections for Internet2. GigaPOP connections are scattered across the United States and provide transmission rates of at least one gigabit per second.

GigaPOP see Gigabit point-of-presence

Gopher one of the first interfaces, or protocols, developed for the Internet. It was widely popular until the advent of HTTP. Gopher protocol is text based, requiring users to navigate by accessing a hierarchical list of files available on a Gopher server.

Harvesters applications that gather metadata, or Web-page descriptors, and create a database of information housed on a separate database server, which is subsequently accessed for Internet Web sites and resources.

Hotspot a public wireless access point primarily serving laptop users. Hotspots are found in airports, hotels, restaurants, and coffee shops. Some hotspots provide free wireless access, while others require a service fee.

HTML see HyperText Markup Language

Hub a hardware product with several connection points that attach multiple independent users to the backbone of a network through one common access point, or port. Hubs typically collect packets, or what are sometimes referred to as chunks of data, from users and transmit them to a local area network or the Internet. Hubs receive and broadcast returned data to all attached users until the correct user collects it. A switching hub, more commonly known as a switch, has the functionality to read destination addresses of each packet and deliver it to the intended user, without broadcasting to all connected users.

HyperText Markup Language a formatting language developed to indicate how documents should display on the Web through the use of markup tags, or elements. There is a finite set of tags and rules for using them in the creation of Web pages. HTML has the recommendation of the World Wide Web Consortium (W3C) and can be interpreted by the majority of Web browsers.

I2 see Internet2

IMS A metadata schema developed by vendors and institutions of higher education for open market–based standards for online learning. The initials *IMS* no longer stand for anything.

Infrared port a communication port using a visual signal instead of wires or cables. Infrared ports are found on computers, motion detectors, PDAs, and a variety of other hardware, and are also used in wireless communications.

Internet Protocol a communications protocol based on the assignment of a unique numerical address, called an IP address, which uniquely identifies each computer on a network and enables accurate data transmissions between computers on the Internet.

Internet Protocol Address a unique identification number assigned to each computer or machine on a network or the Internet. The IP address is currently composed of four groups of decimal numbers separated by periods. The information represented by the numerical code are the Internet network number assigned to an organization; the subnet number, which helps identify separate sections within an organization; and the local machine number, which identifies one computer or machine on the network or Internet.

Internet2 a collaborative effort among institutes of higher education to develop advanced Internet technologies to support Web-based learning and research applications. A major component of I2 is to add sufficient network infrastructure to support real-time multimedia and high-bandwidth interconnections.

Interoperability the capacity of various types of computers, networks, operating systems, and applications to communicate effectively without the need for user intervention to modify settings or load additional applications.

IP see Internet Protocol

IP address see Internet Protocol Address

Java programming language being used more frequently to enhance Web sites through the use of animation, mouseovers (text that pops up when you place the mouse over a word or image), and scrolling text. Java contains small programs or "applets" that are downloaded as part of a Web page. These applets can be safely downloaded through the Internet, can be run immediately without fear of viruses, and are platform independent.

Kerberos an authentication system providing for the secure transmission of information between a user and a server being accessed. Kerberos systems create session keys called tickets, which are embedded in transmissions between one user and a server that links the transmissions to that specific user.

Knowledge base a centralized repository for an organization's information, solutions to issues, best practices, and other data. Information is organized into meaningful categories, which can be queried, enhanced, or used as a basis for training or analysis and can be accessed by either the organization or the general public. DSpace, developed by MIT, is an example of a knowledge base.

LAN see Local Area Network

LDAP see Lightweight Directory Access Protocol

Liberty Alliance a consortium of identity-based vendors and consumer services established to create an open standard for single sign-on authentication. The Alliance offers specifications and guidelines to help resolve technology and business issues with single sign-on authentication while offering users the option to select and manage the use of their identity information.

Lightweight Directory Access Protocol a network-accessible database containing user authentication and authorization information to validate users and their rights to network resources. One advantage of LDAP is that maintenance occurs on one database and is reflected throughout the network.

Link Resolvers using OpenURL syntax, link resolvers receive requests for links to information such as full-text journal articles, compare the link against a set of rules, and return a list of possible resources or targets. SFX and Link Source are commercial examples of link resolvers.

Listserv is L-Soft International, Inc.'s software application for managing email lists, which provides the dissemination of a single message simultaneously to a group of people. Using the email address of the list, participants send their messages to a central server that automatically distributes the message to all subscribers on the list. Other electronic mailing list software applications include Majordomo lists and Procmail lists.

Local Area Network a group of computers and peripherals networked within a small geographical area such as an office building or a small group of buildings such as a university campus with no branches.

Macro a shortcut key that initiates a series of keystrokes and instructions to automate commonly used commands. Macros are user created through the recording of a series of keystrokes and assigning the action to a key, or are packaged as part of a software program. Once created, macros can be used repeatedly.

Markup the process of inserting element descriptors or tags within data to determine how a Web page is displayed or printed.

Metadata used to describe indexing information about a digitized image. The types of elements listed as metadata include intellectual content of an image, digital representation data, and security or management information.

Metasearch the ability to find Web sites by searching across multiple search engines simultaneously. Results are usually displayed in a list with reference to which search engine provided the result. Commercial vendors offering this service include MuseSearch and MetaLib.

Microsoft Passport a single sign-on authentication system developed by Microsoft that enables users to browse between participating Web sites or services without reauthentication. User information is stored on a central Microsoft server.

National Information Standards Organization a nonprofit association formed to develop technical standards for information services, libraries, and publishers. The National Information Standards Organization also maintains and publishes technical standards for existing technologies as well as developing technologies. Experts and practitioners from the fields of publishing, libraries, information technology, and media services serve on committees and serve as officers of the organization.

National Science Digital Library a digital library formed to support science education on all levels and showcase notable resource collections and services. The National Science Digital Library also serves as an example for science educators committed to digital library-enabled science education and is considered the leader in innovation in the application of digital libraries to education.

Network Interface Card a computer expansion card used to connect machines to a network. There are different types of network interface cards designed to work with various types of networks, such as Ethernet, token ring, or FDDI.

NIC see Network Interface Card

NISO see National Information Standards Organization

NSDL see National Science Digital Library

OAI see Open Archives Initiatives

OAI Harvester a harvester utilizing the OAI-PMH framework. The harvester gathers metadata from digital repositories and places it into a database residing on an external server.

OAI–PMH see Open Archives Initiatives Protocol for Metadata Harvesting

OAIster a project of the University of Michigan Digital Library Production Services designed to collect freely available but difficult-to-access academically oriented digital materials and make them available from one Web site. Users are able to search for information on a broad range of topics, view catalog record information about the material, and retrieve a Web-based digital representation of the original work.

OLAC see Open Language Archives Community

Open Archives Initiatives an initiative promoting storing materials, such as research projects, non-peer-reviewed literature, and peer-reviewed papers, through a predefined set of technical mechanisms and assuring interoperability among collections. The OAI has developed standards to provide an alternative to an existing scholarly communication model—that is, third-party publishers—and offers authors the framework for self-archiving, or digitizing, of their own research.

Open Archives Initiatives Protocol for Metadata Harvesting a protocol established by the Open Archives Initiatives providing the method for external harvesters to collect metadata descriptors from digitized material collections housed on separate servers. Once collected, the metadata is used to provide indexing to the harvested collections and materials.

Open Language Archives Community a partnership of individuals and institutions worldwide whose purpose is to create a virtual library of language resources through the development of interoperable standards for digitizing language resources.

Open Source any software whose code is intended to be freely available for modification or improvements and redistributed without any restrictions.

OpenURL a URL that has a structured format that includes information such as volume, issue, and pagination of an article within a digitized journal, allowing for more precise linking.

P2P see Peer-to-Peer

Packet when data is transmitted over a network, it is broken down into chunks of information called packets. Breaking down the communication into smaller units increases the transmission-rate process.

Parse the process of breaking down a command or string of characters into smaller parts so that an application can manage them. The word *parse* also is used to define the process of a Web spider breaking down a Web document into words and phrases to extract keywords and links.

PDA see Personal Digital Assistant

Peer-to-Peer a networking program, such as Napster or Gnutella, that provides a Web-based network, permitting users to share programs, files, network bandwidth, and storage without utilizing a centrally controlled server.

Perl see Practical Extraction and Report Language

Personal Digital Assistant also known as a handheld computer. Small mobile devices providing limited computing and information-storage capabilities. Normally, PDAs include an address book, schedule calendar, to-do lists, and a notepad. Popular PDAs include Palm Zire, Sony Clie, Handspring Treo, and BlackBerry.

Point of Presence see POP

POP refers to either Point of Presence or Post Office Protocol. Point of Presence is a connection point for network access. Post Office Protocol refers to the method used to retrieve e-mail from a mail server.

Port a connection socket located on the back of computers that is used to connect a monitor, a keyboard, a mouse, a printer, and other devices. *Port* also refers to a specific server program on a computer in a network. These services are represented numerically and are part of the URL, appearing after a colon, right after the domain name. Port numbers range from 0 to 65536. The higher-level applications use preassigned port numbers. For example, HTTP services have been assigned port 80.

Portal a Web site that markets itself as a gateway to the Internet. These Web sites encourage users to customize the site with favorite Web links and set the site as their home page. Typically portals present a directory of popular Web sites, a search engine, and other Web-based services, such as free e-mail or weather forecasts.

Post Office Protocol see POP

Practical Extraction and Report Language an open-source programming language designed especially for processing text. It has become widely used in Web interfaces for the creation of interactive forms.

Protocol a set of standardized rules and procedures that computers use to communicate with each other. Protocols enable packets of data to be disassembled and rearranged for quicker transmission rates and then, based on the protocol rules, reassembled at the destination point. Some of the common protocols include TCP/IP and HTTP.

QoS see Quality of Service

Quality of Service supplies the framework for prioritizing certain types of transmissions, reserving bandwidth for certain time periods or special events, and provides different levels of quality based on which type of data you want to transmit. QoS measures network and Internet transmission rates, error rates, and other characteristics to guarantee a specific level of service.

Radio Frequency Identification a small disk containing circuitry, programmed with brief identification information and an antenna, that responds to a corresponding radio frequency signal. Radio frequency identification tags come in a variety of sizes and have been used in place of bar codes because of their greater capacity for storing data, their ability to be reprogrammed, and because they do not require line of sight, like a light pen, to be read.

Regular Expression a term used to describe specific patterns of text. Commonly used when editing text.

Reader Software utilizing a scanner, software that converts scanned typescript materials into synthesized speech. Text can be read immediately, saved as a computer file, or prepared for Braille production. Openbook, Kurzweil 1000, and Cicero Text Reader are popular reader software.

RFID see Radio Frequency Identification

Roaming Service the ability of an access point to automatically pick up users who have moved into its area of service, without any disruption in connectivity. Users freely roam within their own network but can also roam across to adjacent networks.

Router a hardware device situated at the gateway between two networks receiving data packets and routing each packet forward along on the best route based on current network information. Routers also store tables of potential routes with availability information and use this information to determine the best route for a given data packet.

SAN see Storage Area Network

SASL see Simple Authentication and Security Layer

Screen-Magnification Software software enabling users to modify computer screen settings by enlarging images and text size and editing color contrast and color selections. Popular magnification products include ZoomText, MAGic, and Microsoft Accessibility.

Screen readers software that recognizes text displayed on a computer screen and speaks the content. Examples of commercial products include JAWS, Window Eyes, and Hal.

Script a set of instructions for an application written in a simple programming language, such as PERL, that can be executed without user-supplied keystrokes. Because another program, rather than a computer processor, interprets scripts, they do not need to be compiled.

Secure Socket Layer a technology developed by Netscape to allow secure transmissions of private information over the Internet. The connection between a user and a Web site is encrypted so that only the intended parties can read transmitted data, such as credit card numbers. Users know when they connect to a secure Web site because the URLs begin with "https" instead of the customary "http."

Server a computer on a network dedicated to delivering services or resources that are requested by multiple users, or clients. In the client/server model, *server* refers to a software program that waits and responds to requests from its clients.

SGML see Standard Generalized Markup Language

Shibboleth an upshot of Internet2, this initiative is to facilitate interinstitutional, or federated, authentication and authorization for access to content providers, Web pages, government agencies, and so forth. In lieu of traditional user-specific information being used to authenticate, permissions are standards based; for example, authentication based on a course-specific group of students instead of each enrolled student.

Simple Authentication and Security Layer used in conjunction with a connection-based protocol like LDAP, this method adds a layer of protection to the authentication process. Any information passed during the connection process is negotiated via a secure layer. Once a connection is established, this protocol has the option to negotiate a secure channel for subsequent server requests.

Single Sign-On a mechanism permitting user authentication to multiple servers with just one login. Although very handy for users, there is an increased security risk associated with having one password authenticate multiple locations.

Speech Recognition Software enables users to input data by speaking text or commands instead of keying input into a computer. Examples of commercial products include Dragon Naturally Speaking and ViaVoice.

Spyware software secretly bundled with free software or programs that is used to gather information about users and subsequently pass it on to other commercial vendors. Spyware has become part of the public's concern for maintaining privacy on the Internet.

SSL see Secure Socket Layer

SSO see Single Sign-on

Standard Generalized Markup Language a standard for defining a particular set of markup tags or elements in a markup language, such as HTML and XML. Encoded Archival Description (EAD) and Document Type Definition (DTD) are sets of SGML-based tags.

Storage Area Network a hardware device providing network-accessible disk storage space used by individuals or data servers. Information is stored on the SAN instead of on hard drives located in personal computers or data servers.

Switch similar to a hub, a piece of hardware connecting multiple users to a network. Switches transmit outgoing data packets and channel incoming data packets to a specific user.

Sync an abbreviation for *synchronization*, and commonly used to describe the process of comparing databases on a PDA with those contained on a PC and the modification of information to make the two databases identical.

Tablet PC a wireless personal computer similar in size and thickness to a yellow notepad. Tablet PCs have two methods for inputting information, a keyboard and a touch screen. Using a stylus or digital pen, users write on the touch screen, making it possible to store and edit as well as index, search, and share handwritten information via e-mail or cell phone.

Tag an element descriptor used by formatting languages such as HTML, XML, or SGML. Tags are distinguishable from data because they are surrounded by angle brackets (< and >). Tags are interpreted by Web browsers, which in turn format Web pages for display.

Tcl see Tool Command Language

TLS see Transport Layer Security Protocol

Token Ring used to describe computer nodes connecting in a circular pattern. For one computer to communicate with another node, it must pass a token, or a packet of specific information, to the next node, which passes it on to the next node as it travels around the ring, and eventually throughout the network. If one computer breaks a token ring, the network can no longer communicate.

Tool Command Language a programming language used primarily for issuing commands to an interactive program, very similar to Expect. It can be used in Unix, Windows, or Macintosh environments.

Transport Layer Security Protocol the latest enhancement to Secure Socket Layer, version 3.0. This protocol provides a secure layer for clients to access server applications without the threat of interception of information passed between a client and server applications.

Trunk the location or switching center where two large capacity transmission links are connected. All transmissions are direct from point to point, with no additional subdivisions or nodes.

Uniform Resource Locator the addressing system used for naming files that are accessed through the World Wide Web. A URL is composed of the protocol used to connect to the resource, the domain name of the specific server where the file is stored, and the pathname to the information on the target server.

UNIX the most common operating system used on Internet servers. It supports multiuser and multitasking operations. There are many versions of UNIX, and almost every hardware vendor offers its own proprietary version. An offshoot of

UNIX that is increasing in popularity is LINUX, available either as freeware or for purchase commercially.

URL see Uniform Resource Locator

Virtual Private Network authorized remote users are provided access to their organization's private network by way of the public Internet. A secured path or tunnel within the Internet is created to carry encrypted data from an organization's network to a remote user.

Voice over Internet Protocol the process of converting voice, or analog transmissions, into digitized data packets, transferring them over the Internet, and delivering them to their destination in their original configuration, the voice.

VoIP see Voice over Internet Protocol

VPN see Virtual Private Network

W3C see World Wide Web Consortium

WAN see Wide Area Network

Web Services applications that are accessible using the standard Internet protocol of HTTP. The applications provide value-added services and components. Examples include airline reservations, citation databases, and retail Web sites that allow searching, registering, purchasing, and e-mail delivery of items all from one Web site.

Wide Area Network term used to describe a network consisting of two or more local area networks that serves a larger geographical area, such as a large, multibranched university campus.

Wi-Fi see Wireless Fidelity

Wireless Fidelity used to describe a wireless local area network that utilizes the 802.11b standard. This standard operates in the 2.4GHz range with transmission rates up to 11 megabits per second.

World Wide Web Consortium an international Web and Internet consortium of companies. The intention of the consortium is to shape open technologies of the Web so it develops in a single direction rather than having multiple stand-alone functionalities. The technologies include guidelines, specifications, software, and tools.

XML see eXtensible Markup Language

XSL see eXtensible Stylesheet Language

Z39.50 a **National Information Standards Organization** communications protocol used by online public access catalogs to provide searching and retrieval of bibliographic data from other library catalogs and online databases.

Z39.88 a **National Information Standards Organization** standard for the syntax used to create Web-transportable data packets of metadata and other identifiers used to describe an information object, and is the foundation of the context-sensitive, or OpenURL, technology.

INDEX

ABOUT THE EDITOR
AND CONTRIBUTORS

CHARLY BAUER is Product Manager, Metadata Harvesting, at OCLC. He is implementing services that harvest metadata from libraries, museums, and other cultural organizations based on the Open Archives Initiative Protocol and other, similar protocols. Before joining OCLC, he worked at the Ohio Library and Information Network (OhioLINK) as Assistant Director of Library Systems—Multimedia Databases. His primary interest is in shared, multi-institutional services.

MARK CAIN is Chief Information Officer, Cincinnati State Technical and Community College, Cincinnati, Ohio.

H. FRANK CERVONE is the Assistant University Librarian for Information Technology at the Northwestern University Library. He has 20 years of experience in managing information-technology services, the majority of which has been in academic libraries. The author of numerous articles and four books on topics related to information technology, he has been an invited speaker at library information-technology conferences in the United States, Canada, Great Britain, Australia, and Brazil. He has an MSEd with a specialization in online teaching and learning from the California State University, and an MA in information technology management from DePaul University.

NANCY COURTNEY is Coordinator of Outreach and Learning for the Humanities and Social Sciences at the Ohio State University Libraries.

She coordinated the Library Services and Technology Act (LSTA)-funded seminar entitled *Technology for the Rest of Us: What Every Librarian Should Understand about the Technologies That Affect Us* held in Columbus, Ohio, May 24–27, 2004, that formed the basis of this volume. She holds a BA in classics from Northwestern University and an MS in library and information science from the University of Illinois.

WALT CRAWFORD is Senior Analyst at RLG. A library-systems professional since 1968, Crawford is also active in the Library and Information Technology Association (LITA) division of the American Library Association and is a writer and speaker within the library field.

WILFRED (CALL ME "BILL") DREW, JR. is Systems/Reference Librarian at Morrisville College Library. He has taught and written extensively on using the Internet, wireless local area networks in libraries, and the World Wide Web. He is the owner of the Wireless Librarian Web site and the LibWireless e-mail list. He has an MS in Library Science from Drexel University, a BS in Wildlife Biology from Cornell University, and an AS from Tompkins Cortland Community College. He is a recipient of the Chancellor's Award for Excellence in Librarianship and is a past president of the SUNY Librarians Association. Bill also serves as chair of the SUNY ALPEH Users Group.

DARLENE FICHTER is the Coordinator of Data Library Services at the University of Saskatchewan Library. She is also the owner of Northern Lights Internet Solutions, Ltd., a Web-consulting and training company. Darlene is particularly interested in the areas of human-computer interaction, usability testing, and designing positive user experiences. She has been a consultant and project manager for several Web site, portal, digital library, and intranet projects. Darlene is also columnist for *Online* magazine and a frequent conference speaker about new and emerging information technologies.

DR. SAMANTHA K. HASTINGS joined the faculty at the University of North Texas in Denton in 1995. She holds an MLIS from the University of South Florida Tampa and a PhD from Florida State. Sam's research interests in the retrieval of digital images, telecommunications, and evaluation of networked information services influence how she views the changing roles for information professionals. "Without library and information scientists, there is little hope that people will be able to find the information and knowledge needed to flourish in the digital environment." Sam tries to integrate real-world experiences as reflected by teamwork and product development in all of her classes, which range from indexing and abstracting to telecommunications. She directs the digital image management program of study at the School of Library and Information Sciences. She is the current president of the American Society for Information Science and Technology, her favorite professional society.

JERRY HENSLEY is Desktop Software Specialist, Computing and Telecommunications Services, Wright State University, Dayton, Ohio.

ELISE C. LEWIS is a doctoral student in information science at the University of North Texas. Her research interests are in how people interact with 3-D images on the Web and the development of standards for the display and manipulations of the images. She is manager of the Digital Imaging Lab at the School of Library and Information Sciences, research fellow for the Texas Center for Digital Knowledge, and teaching assistant for the advanced digital-imaging classes.

ROBERT E. MOLYNEUX is Chief Statistician at Sirsi Corporation. He has worked on and with computers for a number of years, including work on the Internet in the days before the mouse and the Web.

ART RHYNO is a Systems Librarian at the University of Windsor (Ontario, Canada) and since the late 1990s has been an advocate for the use of XML and open-source software in libraries.

FRANCES RICE is Head of Information Technology at the Roesch Library, University of Dayton, in Dayton, Ohio. Her main responsibilities are planning, implementing, and maintaining emerging library technologies.

ERIC H. SCHNELL is an Associate Professor and Head of Information Technology at the John A. Prior Health Sciences Library at the Ohio State University.

SARAH L. SHREEVES is the Coordinator for the Illinois Digital Environment for Access to Learning and Scholarship at the University of Illinois Library at Urbana-Champaign. Previously she served as project coordinator for two Open Archives Initiative based projects at the University of Illinois: the Institute of Museum and Library Services funded Digital Collections and Content Project from 2002–2005 and the Andrew W. Mellon Foundation funded Illinois Open Archives Initiative Metadata Harvesting Project from 2001–2002. From 1992 until 2001 she worked in the Massachusetts Institute of Technology Libraries. She has a BA in Medieval Studies from Bryn Mawr College, an MA in Children's Literature from Simmons College, and an MS in Library and Information Science from the University of Illinois at Urbana-Champaign.

KATHLEEN M. WEBB is an Associate Professor and Interim Dean of Roesch Library, University of Dayton. Kathy received her MLS from UCLA and her undergraduate degree from Pennsylvania State University. Kathy has been at the University of Dayton for 11 years and has worked in Government Documents, Reference, and Instruction. Kathy led the library's first Web-development effort in 1995 and continues to lead the Web Committee. Kathy has been a member of the OhioLINK User Services Committee since 1998 and was involved in launching OhioLINK's chat reference service.